CW01476872

This book provides a detailed and readable account of all types of camping. It aims to help the would-be camper to decide what sort of holiday will suit him best and to select the right equipment. The various tents available are dealt with fully, as are trailer tents, caravans and motor caravans. The book advises on the choice of accessories, on food and cooking in camp, and on the maintenance and repair of equipment. It also discusses camping abroad, insurance, what to look for in a site and how to pitch, and describes some suitable tours for beginners both at home and abroad. The text is illustrated throughout.

THE AUTHOR

Eric Dominy has camped for many years, his experience varying from school and cadet camps to luxury camping in large family frame tents. At present, he camps regularly with his family and instructs on arduous training, being Duke of Edinburgh Award Scheme Officer with his cadet contingent.

TEACH YOURSELF BOOKS
CAMPING

ERIC DOMINY

TEACH YOURSELF BOOKS
ST. PAUL'S HOUSE WARWICK LANE LONDON EC4

First printed 1972

Copyright © 1972
The English Universities Press Ltd.

ISBN 0 340 04672 4

PRINTED AND BOUND IN ENGLAND
FOR THE ENGLISH UNIVERSITIES PRESS LTD
BY HAZELL WATSON AND VINEY, AYLESBURY

Contents

Acknowledgements

I wish to thank Laurie Watson of the London Judo Society for his help and advice in respect of lightweight camping and Captain Roger Hedgecoe of the Christ's College Finchley Contingent of the Combined Cadet Force for permission to use his notes and drawings of the emergency "bivi" he devised for use on the Unit's arduous training. It has been used successfully on night exercises, and the cadets have found it warm and comfortable. Both Laurie Watson and Roger Hedgecoe were most helpful with their comments on the avoidance and treatment of exposure.

My thanks are also due to Peter Johnson who produced the excellent illustrations that appear throughout this book.

Eric Dominy

Introduction

Trends and fashions in camping, just as in anything else, change with the times. When I started camping, many years ago, you took a train to the station nearest the site where you proposed to camp and then walked or cycled to the site itself, carrying your tent and all other necessaries on your back. The public image of a camper was a scruffy, unshaven individual who crawled into and out of a tiny army-type bivouac tent – a bell-tent was real luxury because you could stand up in the middle without rubbing your hair on the canvas. This was not far from the truth, and it is still the impression of British camping and campers held on the Continent, even though it is totally wrong today. To obtain an up-to-date picture of British camping you have only to visit a camping site in the United Kingdom or to see British campers abroad – first-class modern tents and equipment are apparent everywhere. These tents not only provide every comfort but are also a picturesque addition to the countryside. Camping is now fashionable and articles on the subject frequently appear in the quality national press.

Campers, however, have always attempted to make their lives under canvas more comfortable. We used to cut bracken for a bed – and remarkably comfortable this sort of bed can be – hung up a cycle lamp on the ridge pole, wrapped our boots in our sweaters for a pillow and used an old blanket instead of a sleeping bag. Cooking was done on a wood fire, using a tripod of sticks to suspend a cooking pot (I always managed to allow one of the legs of the tripod to catch fire, and had to rescue my pot from the fire and my meal from the ashes). Nowadays, bottled gas provides heat for cooking and warmth and light for reading. Visit my family in its modern frame tent and you will find over six feet of headroom, two separate bedrooms and a living space, and a gas stove for cooking; a gas fire is used if it is cold and a fluorescent electric tube provides light, drawing current from the car battery. Many lightweight campers disparage the comfort of frame tents, but I fail to see why anyone with sufficient car space to carry a large tent and equipment should not do so; I cannot see any virtue in unnecessary discomfort.

If you wish to persuade your wife to join you on a camping holiday, especially for a second time, provide her with every convenience and do not load her with all the housework or tent work. My first family camping expedition took place a few years after the War and saw us visit Belgium and France. The first night we camped in the Belgian sand dunes, and the soft sand provided many problems in tent pitching and further difficulties in digging out the car the next morning. We also had trouble in obtaining paraffin ("petrole" in French) and then were not sure whether it was actually paraffin or petrol that we had been given. On another occasion we were awakened by the morning sun to find the site, both inside and outside the tent, overrun by hundreds of tiny field mice. I have a further recollection of pitching the tent in the dark and rain on a tractor track on a farm (with permission obtained in my best, almost non-existent, French) using a haystack as a shelter from the weather. Looking back, all this was great fun, but it was many years before I could persuade my wife to camp again. Now, somewhat older, we camp on established sites, often provided with a small general store and hot showers, and almost without exception with flush toilets.

The tents to be seen are many and varied. The choice is almost unlimited – so wide, in fact, that it is very difficult to come to a decision when buying. Fortunately, however, bad tents are few and far between. Your best bet is to visit a large exhibition and choose the type which is most suitable to you in both size and price; I will discuss this at some length in a later chapter.

You can learn about camping at evening institutes or at courses arranged by the Central Council of Physical Recreation. You should make enquiries about the former at your local education office. The address of the Central Council of Physical Recreation will be found amongst the useful addresses at the end of this book.

Part One

Let's Go Camping

Chapter 1

Why Camping Holidays?

I am often asked why I enjoy camping, and I think it is because of the freedom it provides. You can camp in any way you choose – in tents of every shape and size, or in a caravan, or go half-way and use a trailer tent. You can make it tough by carrying your tent and all your equipment on your back, or you can travel by car and use a luxury tent. You can trail a caravan behind your car or hire a huge, static 'van on a chosen site. You can go where you like when you like. If it is wet in the west, you go to the east – no advance booking problems. You get up at whatever time you wish and dress as you like for breakfast. The dining room is never closed and your favourite meal is always available. No notice says "All rooms must be vacated by 10.00 a.m. each day". If you don't like your neighbours or if the children next door are noisy, you can move. Above all, camping is cheap once you have your equipment. You can travel far afield in Europe at a cost which is very much less than a hotel holiday comparatively near home.

The choice of sites is a matter for the individual. My family and I base our plans on personal recommendations. We also read camping magazines for reports on sites and plan our route; but it is seldom that we do not meet someone coming in the opposite direction at our first site who can advise on sites and routes to be used or avoided. This is very helpful, as what was first-class on a site visited in

June may be entirely different if you visit the same site when it is overcrowded in August. Personally, I always find the sites run by the local councils to be amongst the best. As a rule, the council are not out to make a large profit, and they have the goodwill of both local people and visitors to consider.

If you are a lover of comfort, you cannot really get an idea of how comfortable camping can be without visiting a site; modern gadgets have made it possible for the well-equipped person or family to have a luxury holiday and a camping holiday at the same time. The days of slackening guys at night are gone and you no longer touch the material of the tent when you stand up. Your bed is, or should be, as comfortable and warm as that at home, and you can cook on gas using non-stick pots and pans. But you still have all the advantages of a camping holiday. A lightweight camper can carry a first-class tent, in addition to a warm sleeping bag and an air bed, if he selects from the goods offered at reasonable prices by the specialist manufacturers. Strictly speaking, you are confined to camping on sites or on private land with permission, but neither I nor any of my friends who camp or climb have been disturbed while pitched in isolated places. The main thing is to leave no mess – the only trace of your site should be a patch of slightly faded grass.

Published statistics show that Britain has some two million campers (only a third of those in France) and in every country the movement towards camping holidays grows. A survey made by the Camping Trades Association shows that the average camper is aged forty-five, has a wife and two children, is in a profession or a technical job and has been camping for over ten years. He camps because he likes open air and independence. He travels in a car, has a frame tent, uses a sleeping bag and an air bed instead of a camp bed, cooks on gas and uses a tent light powered by his car battery. He likes to use a site provided with a shop and laundry facilities. He usually spends his holidays camping abroad, but camps in the United Kingdom at weekends. Well, there you have a picture of the average camper. If you are not yet a camper, this gives you a good idea of the people you will meet at any site that you select.

The word "camper" is now used to include people who tour and live in tents of all types, trailer tents, trailer caravans and motor caravans. You are a camper whether you travel on foot, or cycle or drive from site to site in a Rolls and in most cases you are equally welcome. This is just as it should be.

Chapter 2

What Type of Camping?

You have an infinite choice: tents of all shapes, sizes and weights, trailer tents, trailer caravans and motor caravans. I am inclined to agree with the "old-timers" who say that the only true form of camping is that practised by the young and enthusiastic who carry their tents and equipment on their backs or perhaps on bicycles, but this is not in keeping with modern conditions. Although I am aware that girls go potholing and participate in most active pursuits, my advice to male camping enthusiasts is not to expect your wife or girl-friend to participate in lightweight camping. The next step up is the large ridge tent with a ridge pole or the smaller frame tent; in the former you can stand up in the centre under the ridge pole, whilst you can stand up almost anywhere in the latter without ducking your head. From this stage you move to larger frame tents as your family increases.

Trailer tents fold down into comparatively small trailers which are far easier to tow than caravans. They open up easily, or comparatively easily, into tents, the main advantages being that it takes less time to erect them than a frame tent and that the beds, usually bunks, are well off the ground, the bedroom being in the trailer itself.

The next step forward in comfort is the trailer caravan, which can vary in size from a 'van no bigger than a baggage trailer to a huge home on wheels remaining permanently on a site. The range of price is as wide as that of size, but your main consideration when choosing a caravan must always be the ability of your car to tow the 'van. Whereas the thing to avoid when buying a tent is selecting one too small for your family, with a caravan you must not choose one too large for your car.

Rapidly gaining in popularity is the motor caravan. This is a caravan built up on a commercial vehicle chassis, the final effect being a motorised caravan which provides all the comforts of a trailer 'van without the problem of having to tow. There is a disadvantage, however, in that you have to use the vehicle as a private car during the rest of the year, or run a car in addition. If you do use the motor caravan as a car, you must be satisfied with a vehicle whose performance is equivalent to that of a commercial van, for that is really what you are driving.

Although most people who camp – whether in tent, caravan or motor caravan – do so because it is far cheaper than a holiday in a hotel, there is no doubt that the person or family equipping itself from scratch for its first camping holiday is faced with considerable expense. The lightweight camper heading for the mountains may not have to pay so much for his tent as the family man in his big frame tent, but he must have a warm and lightweight sleeping bag, which is expensive, and every part of his equipment must be light and will probably have to be specially purchased. As the lightweight man (or girl) is usually young, money is often in short supply. The frame tent man may well be older and have more money to spare, but frame tents generally cost more than the lightweight variety, and trailer tents, trailer caravans and motor caravans get progressively more expensive. I shall, of course, deal with the various types of tents, the trailer tent, the caravan and the motor caravan, and discuss their advantages and dis-advantages, in the appropriate chapters.

Whatever means of camping you decide to adopt, you must ensure that you are fully equipped for it before you leave. It is easy and a good idea to list all the essentials. A good comprehensive catalogue will help you here, but the only real way of ensuring that nothing vital is missing is to have a trial run. I know one family, who, having purchased their tent and other kit, had a trial week in camp on their garden lawn, including sleeping and cooking in the tent. I did not go as far as this, but I did erect my tent in the garden to check it for faults and missing pieces. Despite this and years of camping experience, I arrived in Wales recently to find myself without a mallet (a large wrench from the car tool kit did the job). Talking of mallets, I find the small, light one supplied with the tent useless and always take a large carpenter's mallet. If you carry your kit, this will, of course, be too large and cumber-some. The lightweight man using "skewer" pegs can drive them home with his hand or with a stone.

It is most important to erect a new tent before setting off on holiday, giving yourself time to collect any missing pieces from your supplier or to change bits which do not fit. In any case, it is better to feel a fool at home as you battle with a frame tent for the first time than to do so on the site in full view of the other campers. As a matter of fact, it is seldom that anyone laughs – usually there is a rush to help – but one can feel ridiculous just the same. On a recent holiday, I turned my tent frame out of its bag and laid it out to find that it was twisted in the middle – one end was the correct way up whilst the other was up-side down, all the frame sections crossing over in the centre. We quickly turned one end over only to find the other end turned over as well, and hard as we tried we could not sort it out. Finally, in desperation, I refolded the frame, put it back in its bag and then tipped it out again; this time it unfolded correctly. I have no idea why or how this was, but it has not happened to me again. Probably we were careless in packing up the tent at our previous site.

The camper's requirements are very much the same whichever method of camping you favour; the first essential is the roof over your head, whether it is a tent, caravan or motor caravan. Having decided which suits you best and obtained it, you then have to look at the long list of items advertised as necessities. Great care must be taken when selecting the accessories – no good camping supplier will push unnecessary items (he probably will not stock them anyway), so it is well worth while going to one of these. Of course, opinions vary as to what is necessary and unnecessary. But, as we all have to sleep and eat on holiday, you will require bedding and cooking equipment. You also have to consider whether you will need to make toilet arrangements. Other accessories are very much a matter of personal choice, and I will discuss what is available in Chapter 6.

Chapter 3

Wives Enjoy Camping As Well –
A Chapter Addressed to the Ladies

It was not so very long ago that, whilst the men of the family enjoyed their camping holiday, it became something of an endurance test for the womenfolk. Cooking was done on a wood fire and the wind would blow smoke all over the cook – no matter on which side of the fire she placed herself. Later we progressed to a spirit or oil stove, which seemed to give insufficient heat and lost what little it did produce with the slightest breeze. The pressure stove certainly provided the necessary heat, but terrified most women. Nowadays, however, we are supplied with twin-burner gas stoves which are clean and easy to use.

If you have any say in the purchase of a stove – and you should see that you have – make sure that you can operate the taps without breaking your fingernails. Also think of the safety position; some cookers seem designed to slide off metal cooking tables and the tables themselves are often unstable, making them a death trap for small children or dogs if you take them. It is much better to cook on or near the floor, sitting on a stool, than to use an unsafe table of "regulation" height.

There will be considerable loss of heat should you attempt to cook in a wind or in cold weather. This loss of heat not only uses up your fuel but also means that it takes much longer to prepare a meal. Some stoves and tables have built-in wind-shields. If you do not have this sort, get your husband to make one or buy one of the types used on the beach.

Do not allow your husband to palm you off with a set of thin lightweight cooking pans. Stronger, thicker pans do not use more gas – rather, they retain heat. Insist also on non-stick pans; they are a godsend at any time, but especially in camp.

A great boon to camp cooks is the mini pressure cooker. A well-known manufacturer produces a small model ideal for campers, and with one of these you can make a first-class meal from the cheaper cuts of meat. The mini-pressure cooker is quite safe, being provided with safety locking lugs and a safety steam valve, and can also be used as an ordinary saucepan should you not want to use it for pressure cooking. The separator inside enables you to cook several different vegetables at the same time.

The wide-mouth types of vacuum flask are extremely useful. Camp cooks often find themselves short of burners and you can use these flasks to keep things warm whilst you are preparing a meal. They also enable you to cook meals, particularly stews and soups, at a time convenient to you.

An ample supply of polythene bags is a must. These are used for vegetables, to pack up shoes, to wrap wet clothing in when moving on to another site and so on. You should also ensure that you have some securely sealing plastic containers for jam, butter, etc.

A large bag or box for use as a waste bin is an essential in the tent. Unless you provide one it will be impossible to keep the tent tidy, especially when you have children with you. I object to living in a pigsty and I am sure you do too.

If you want the children to help you cook, always look as if you enjoy it. As long as they have this impression, even though it may be totally false, they will compete to help or perhaps take over entirely. It is really surprising how well they will do, even if they are left completely alone to get on with it.

As far as food is concerned we like to shop locally and, within reason, to buy the produce of the area. I say within reason because we drew the line in Barcelona when invited to select our dinner from amongst a few dozen octopi swimming round a tank, and we have declined other local delicacies on similar occasions. It is worth looking around for some everyday items in wrapping specially suitable for campers. For example, you can buy butter in strong, greaseproof cartons complete with lid. We also go for marmalade in a screw top jar; this makes it far more ant- and wasp-proof. Local wines are often first-class and usually cheap.

When abroad I am sure you will find that children will master foreign currency and metric weights far faster than you can yourself. If you give them the freedom of the supermarket with some idea of what you require and a fairly limited supply of cash, you will find that the result is very satisfactory. Of course, you will have to watch them with the cream cakes, otherwise you will be putting on weight.

Milk is a great problem. You either run out at an essential moment or find that it has turned sour. It is usually possible to buy fresh milk in the morning from the camp shop or from the local milkman who calls, but, unless you have some means of keeping it cool, it must be used immediately it is obtained. We have fresh milk with our cereal at breakfast and use powdered milk for drinks.

It is very difficult to decide what clothing to take camping. You want to look nice, but space is limited. I pack for myself and leave my wife to look after herself and the children. I usually read her the Riot Act about taking far too much, but somehow I always manage to take a substantial amount for myself. Seriously though, ordinary campers do attempt to pack far too much clothing. All you really require are slacks and sweaters – ideal for camp life – and a respectable dress for town visits. Do not be ashamed to take a hot water bottle. It makes a great difference on cold nights and it is surprising how chilly a fine summer night can be.

Finally, if your family are trying to persuade you to go camping for the first time, my advice is go, but make sure that your tent is sufficiently large and that you have gas available for cooking.

Part Two

Equipment

Chapter 4

Which Tent and All About It

If you have made up your mind to do your camping in a tent, your next decision is—which tent? Although there is a wide selection of tents on the market, your choice is restricted to a large extent by the type of transport to be used, the number of people it is proposed to house in the tent and the money available to pay for it. Transport can vary from your own two feet to the very large limousine, and the difference between the types of tents is just about as great.

Readers of my book *Camping at Home and Abroad* will already know that I greatly favour hiring a tent for your first camping holiday. As I have mentioned, it is worth going to a good supplier; he will give you sound advice based on practical experience and will not attempt to unload unnecessary kit on you (this also applies to people who wish to purchase equipment). Camping equipment hirers only stock the best equipment; it does not pay them to buy unsatisfactory gear. If you do decide to hire, try to choose a dealer who allows you two or three days at each end of your holiday to collect and return the gear, because if you have to collect on Friday and return on the Monday you may have to pay for two extra weeks' hire, or at least for the extra days. Whilst I have always dealt with one particular firm and found them reliable, it does pay to find a local dealer as hire is not cheap, and added rail charges each way make it more expensive. Many dealers will deduct the hire fee from the cost of a tent if you decide to buy on your return, or allow you a 10 per cent deduction on camping gear hired for a considerable period. Provided, then, that you subsequently buy a tent and choose the right dealer, your hire charges for your entire camping holiday are very reasonable and may perhaps be recovered completely.

A common mistake when choosing a tent is to select one which is too small for your purposes – give yourself plenty of room. You require adequate living and cooking space, especially if the weather is wet, and you do not want your chairs and tables to rub against the tent wall. Ensure that the beds you choose will go into the sleeping compartment of the tent and still allow a little space between them, and also between each bed and the tent wall. Most camp beds are 2 ft wide and, whilst in theory this is all the width you require, you will find it very inconvenient if you have to crawl along the bed to get into the sleeping compartment, and have to stand on it to get dressed and undressed. This places an undue strain on an air bed and is quite a balancing feat on a camp bed; in fact, you are likely to find the bed tipping sideways and throwing you against the wall, which does not greatly improve the tent.

A general guide when selecting a tent for family use is to decide how much sleeping area is required – the living space should be about the same area. In addition, you have the area covered by the awning. This is only my idea, however; opinions vary so much that any rule I might attempt to lay down would be disputed by about 75 per cent of other campers.

Conversely, if you propose to camp alone, do not choose a tent which is too large for you to handle by yourself. Two people can handle a tent of any size when familiar with it, but a lone camper will find it very difficult indeed, and perhaps impossible, to erect a large frame tent.

The variations in size, weight and shape of tent are so great that I will describe each in turn, explaining the advantages and disadvantages of each as they appear to me.

Lightweight Tents Suitable for Hikers and Climbers

1 *The Single Pole Tent*

This looks a bit like a tiny bell tent (see Fig. 1). It is large enough for two people and, whilst it can be purchased in

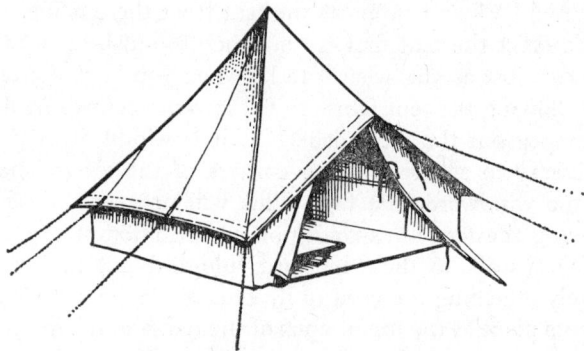

Fig. 1

its basic form, requires a sewn-in groundsheet to complete it; this applies to all tents. You can also obtain a flysheet, which is basically a second layer of canvas separated from the main tent by a gap of about six inches. This is useful in wet weather as it permits you to touch the walls of the tent without bringing water through and to cook in the shelter of the small awning it forms. In addition, a flysheet has the effect of keeping the inside of the tent warm in cold weather and cool when the weather is hot. However, it does add to the weight and bulk to be carried, and is not essential. A good quality lightweight canvas not only has the normal proofing but also withstands damp and rain by the closeness of its weave.

The single pole occupies the centre of the tent. This can be rather a nuisance until you get used to it, but it is no worse than a small ridge tent. In fact, you have far more headroom in the single pole type of tent, and it also provides you with greater comfort and more convenient cooking facilities in bad weather. If you really object to a central pole, you can obtain an "A" pole which is like an inverted "V" and supports the tent from the outside.

To erect the tent first lay out the groundsheet. Pull it out flat, just as you wish it to be when you have the tent up, allowing the tent fabric to fall into the centre. At this stage peg out the groundsheet. If it is windy, it may be necessary to secure the two corners of the groundsheet on the windward side first. This will prevent the wind blowing the tent out of position as you attempt to erect it. Now walk to the windward side and put in a peg, loosely attaching the cord to it. This done, push the pole into its place at the top or apex of the tent and lift it into a perpendicular position, placing the base of the pole into its position on the floor. From here it is easy to insert a peg on the side opposite to that on which the first peg was placed and hook on the cord; this should hold the tent erect whilst you hammer in all the other pegs and secure the cords. If you use an "A" pole instead of the single internal pole, it should be put up at this stage. After you have erected the tent a few times you will know exactly where the first pegs should be placed, and a very short time should elapse between deciding on the site and being fully camped down.

To take down the tent reverse the procedure, making it a habit to unpeg the leeward side first. Try to fold the tent fabric neatly on the groundsheet as, unless you do this, you will be unable to pack the tent up tidily making the smallest possible bundle. As in the case of all types of tents, the erection and dismantling of the tent must be done with door zips closed in order to keep the tent in shape.

2 The Baby Ridge Tent

The ridge tent gets it name from its shape. Looked at from one end it is shaped rather like an inverted "V", coming to a ridge at the top which is supported by guys and a pole at each end (see Fig. 2). The larger models, and some of

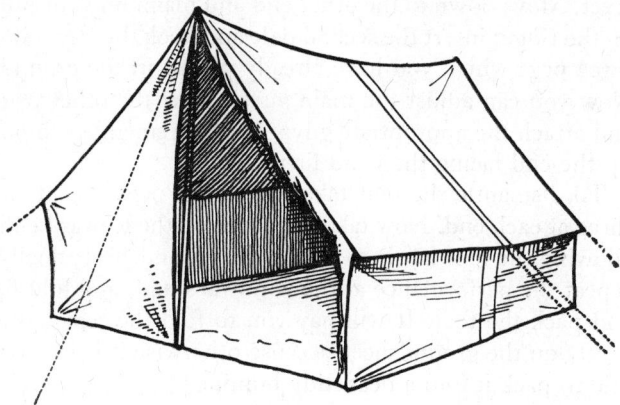

Fig. 2

the smaller if the owner so desires, have a pole running the length of the tent supporting the top; this is known as the ridge pole. It adds weight and bulk to the tent for carrying purposes, but, on the other hand, helps the tent keep its shape and adds a little height in the middle where the unsupported canvas tends to sag. I consider a sewn-in groundsheet essential. Tents of the type suitable for carrying on the back usually measure about 6 ft 6 ins long by up to about 4 ft 6 ins wide and will hold two people. Even smaller ones are available for solo campers.

To erect the tent lay out the groundsheet in the position in which the tent is finally to be pitched. Place the tent on the groundsheet and put three pegs into the ground at each end. These pegs take the guys, which lead to the end of the ridge and the two corners. Hook the guys onto the pegs at the windward end and insert the pole at the same end. The guys pulling one way and a gentle pull on the canvas from yourself at the other end will hold the pole erect. Move down to the other end and maintain your pull on the ridge; insert the second pole and hook the guys onto three pegs which you have already placed in the ground. Now you can adjust the main guys, insert the other pegs and attach the appropriate guys. Always remember to put up the end facing the wind first.

To dismantle the tent take out all the pegs except the three at each end. Now take out those on the leeward end, allowing the tent fabric to fall on the groundsheet; finally, repeat the performance at the windward end, and fold up and pack the tent. It will pay you to fold the tent fabric neatly on the groundsheet because otherwise it is impossible to pack it into a neat, tidy bundle.

Tents Suitable for Cyclists and Motor Cyclists

The cyclist is not much better off for space than the camper who travels on foot. He is certainly able to carry panniers on each side of his rear wheel and to make use of a carrier, but he cannot use a pack, or if he does it must be light in weight to avoid upsetting his balance. A pack also catches the wind.

The motor cyclist is less worried by the problem of weight, but still has a limited carrying capacity – especially if he takes a passenger on his pillion. He might carry a flysheet for his tent or a larger size of ridge tent. Other possibilities are the small frame tent and the pneumatic "Igloo".

Probably the best set-up for campers using two-wheel transport is to team up with other cyclists or motor cyclists. By this means it is possible to carry the slightly larger tent required for four people without much addition to the total bulk; certainly it reduces the bulk carried by each individual person.

1 *The Single Pole or Ridge Tent*
Both these tents, which I have already described, are ideal for the cyclist. They are also suitable for the motor cyclist.

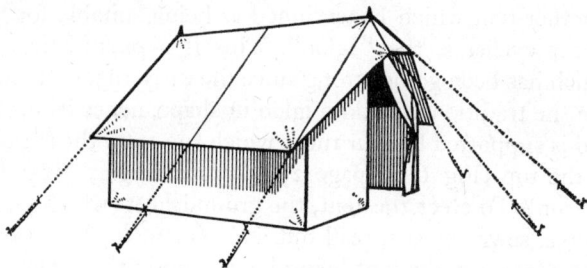

Fig. 3

He will probably carry a flysheet for his tent (see Fig. 3) and may well use a bigger ridge tent, such as that shown in Fig. 4.

For the two people who may be expected to travel on a motor cycle, the recommended floor space is 7 ft × 5 ft, and there should be almost enough height to be able to stand upright. The most likely type of tent to fit this specification is a ridge tent with a flysheet.

Fig. 4

2 *The Pneumatic "Igloo"*

Another tent which I mentioned as being suitable for the motor cyclist is the "Igloo". This is a pneumatic tent which has been going strong since the early 1930s. It looks like the traditional Eskimo igloo in shape, hence its name, and is supported by four tubes which run from the corners to the top (Fig. 6 on page 27 shows a larger, six-sided version). To erect the tent, the groundsheet (which is, of course, sewn in) is spread out and pinned to the ground with tent pegs, the tent being heaped up in the middle of the groundsheet. The tubes are then blown up with a pump to a pressure of about 12 lbs to 14 lbs. Use a car pump – if you attempt to erect the tent with the type of pump supplied for an air mattress, you have a long, hard spell of pumping before the tent is fully erect. The doorway is round, being closed with zip-up flaps. There is no flysheet to the basic tent, although one is obtainable. It is erected on a frame, rather like a second, larger, tent (see Fig. 5). This may seem to be a cumbersome construction and is probably the reason why very few are seen in use. In fact, however, the flysheet is easy to erect. The pole sections are light and simple to put together, and the fabric drops into place without difficulty. The tent weighs 32 lbs approximately, having 6 ft headroom in the centre. The basic model has four sides.

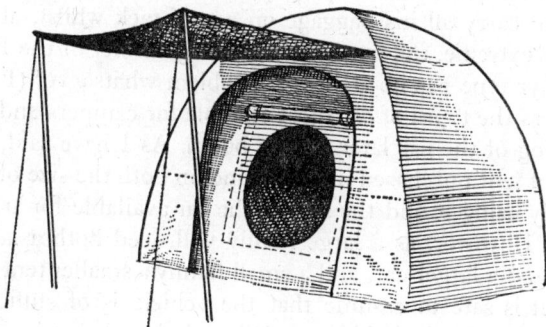

Fig. 5

The tent by itself is waterproof and comfortable. I have also seen the flysheet used by itself, and this appears to be quite satisfactory in good weather. Combined, the "Igloo" and the flysheet provide an almost completely weather-proof holiday home which will withstand most gales and storms.

3 *The Small Frame Tent*
The other possibility for the motor cyclist is the small frame tent. As this consists of an outer tent with an inner

sleeping compartment, it is really the equivalent of carrying a tent with a flysheet and is fairly bulky. I will describe the erection of frame tents later.

In this section I have only discussed the camper on the solo motor cycle; naturally more space is available if a side car is used and the bulk-weight problem is reduced.

Tents Suitable for the Motorist

The ownership, or at least use, of a car does not automatically solve all camping problems. The Mini owner has to carry all his baggage on a roof rack whilst, at the other extreme, the family using a large utility of the Ford Zephyr type has no transport problem whatsoever (I will discuss the types of car most suitable for campers and the loading of the car later in this book). As I have said, the size of tent purchased must depend on both the size of the family using it and the size of the car available for transport. However, as a large family will need both a larger tent and a larger car, and a small family a smaller tent and car, it is safe to assume that the vehicle is of sufficient size to carry a suitable tent. What choice of tent is available?

1 *The Pneumatic "Igloo"*

The later, larger, six-sided model would suit a motorist (see Fig. 6). The floor of the four-sided tent is square, each side being 6 ft 9 ins. This bigger version is naturally even more roomy. I have already described the small tent and its erection fully, and the larger version follows the same lines. The "Igloo" is very reliable and nobody need be put off buying one for fear of punctures or air leakage.

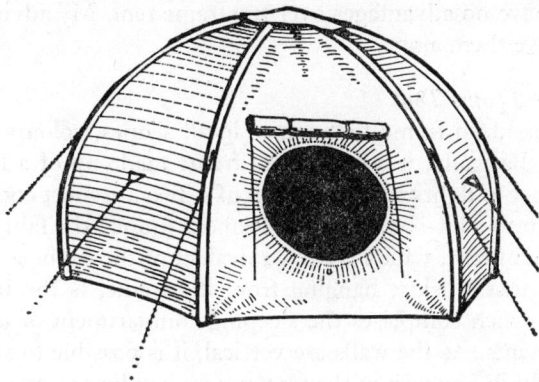

Fig. 6

2 *The Auto-tent*

This was a hotch-potch tent introduced by British manufacturers in an attempt to keep up with the Continentals
when they introduced frame tents. All the additions and
improvements made to ridge tents by enthusiasts were in-
corporated, such as sewn-in groundsheets, bell ends for
storage space, zip openings, awnings and so on (see Fig. 7).
You can still see them on camp sites and a few dealers
include them in their lists. However, they are out of date

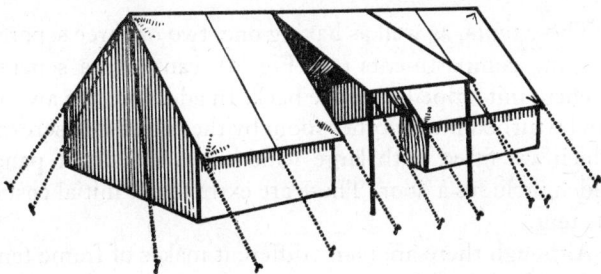

Fig. 7

and have no advantages over the frame tent. My advice is
to leave them alone.

3 *The Frame Tent*

The modern frame tent comes in all shapes, colours and
sizes. Basically, it consists of a frame made up of a large
number of lightweight poles, all of which are short enough
to fit into a kit-bag. Over the frame is draped the fabric of
the main tent, which is the equivalent of the flysheet on a
ridge tent. Inside, hanging from the frame, is the inner
tent, which comprises the sleeping compartment or compartments. As the walls are vertical, it is possible to stand
upright in any part of the tent and no bending or crawling
is necessary (see Fig. 8).

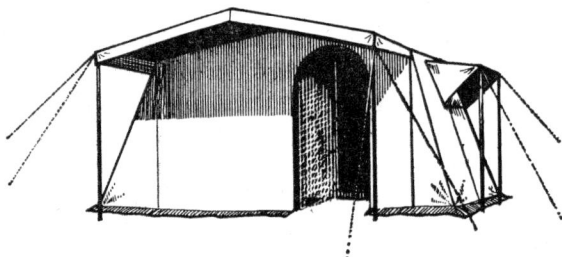

Fig. 8

These tents, as well as having one, two or three separate
sleeping compartments (see Fig. 9), can have a separate
kitchen unit zipped onto the back. In addition, the awning
can be turned into another room by the use of side screens,
which are fitted with large windows, and a front panel,
which includes a door. These are extra to the initial cost of
the tent.

Although there are many different makes of frame tents
and, as I have said, they come in varying shapes and sizes,

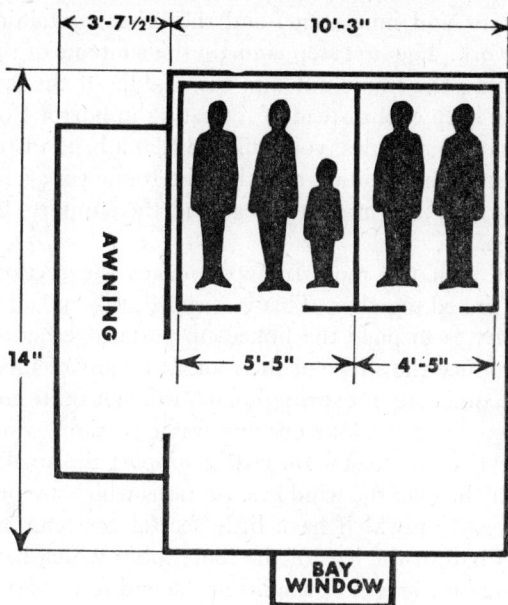

Fig. 9

once you have mastered the construction of one type you should not find much difficulty with others. My experience is that the instructions provided with tents are either non-existent or very brief—they even come in foreign languages. British manufacturers are a little better in this respect, although most manufacturers are, in fact, improving nowadays.

Do not leave the first erection of your tent until you arrive at the site; this will only make you look and feel foolish, and may well spoil your holiday. Instead, choose a windless day and take the tent into the garden. It will have arrived in two bags, one containing the tent fabric (both main tent and inner tent) and the other containing the framework. The first step is to tip the contents of the bag containing the frame out into the middle of the lawn. If you can keep cool instead of retreating in horror from the dozens of short poles, you will find that a brief inspection will clarify the position and that the framework falls into three groups: the roof, the legs and the supports for the awnings.

Start with the roof. In most makes the sections are spring linked together. This is very helpful, and all that is necessary is to push the linked-up parts together, which will produce the shape of the roof. If by any chance your roof sections are not spring linked, it is not quite so easy; but keep calm and take out any frame sections which are thinner than the rest – these will support the small awnings which cover the windows. Sections which are plugged at one end or which have little feet at one end are the bottom half of the legs of the tent; tubes which have adjustments for length or a spike at the end form part of the frame to the awnings. You are now getting quite close to the three groups I mentioned at the beginning. The upper half of the leg will be a straight tube with no attachments. You will have one of these for each leg, so if you sort out four, or six as the case may be, identical tubes you will almost certainly be correct.

You should now be left with the roof section. A good look at the diagram on the instructions, or the illustrations in this book, will show you how the roof section is shaped. The centre sections at each end and the corner sections can be picked out easily, as they have fittings for two or three tubes at different angles and are almost certain to be reinforced. From this you should be able to assemble the roof section, even if it is not spring linked.

By now you have the frame tubes sorted in several heaps. These consist respectively of the roof, the legs of the main tent frame and the awnings sections. This is the time to start putting up the tent. Assemble the roof either by the simple method of putting together the spring linked sections, or by laying out the corners and centre sections in their approximate places and then fitting in the intermediate tubes (see Fig. 10). Now place the legs on the ground at

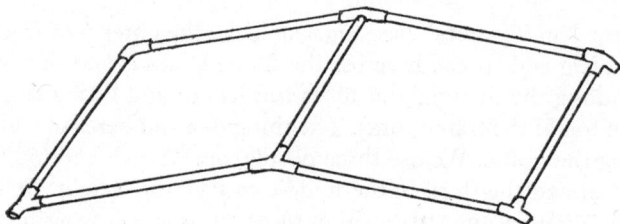

Fig. 10

each corner, and in the centre if you have six or eight legs. Again, the two sections of each leg should be spring linked. Starting at one end, push in the first pair of legs, only raising the tent to half-height. Do this for the centre and then for the end legs. This can be done by one person, but it is easier with two and saves strain on the frame if both sides are raised together.

I know people who put out the groundsheet of the inner tent and link the top of the inner with the framework at this stage. I admit that this saves reaching up, but it does add pressure to the frame as it is raised to its full height and can be difficult should it be windy. I prefer to position the inner tent later.

We have therefore assembled the frame of the roof and raised the frame to half-height; this is called having the

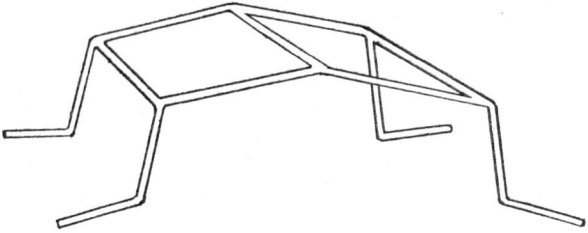

Fig. 11

tent "on its knees" (see Fig.11). Take the outer tent from its bag and spread it across the frame (I always do this by pulling the material out to its full length and lifting it up on top of the framework). The thing to avoid here is bending the frame. We use three people, one at each end to lift it on and the third in the middle to take the weight. Fold the material into its position on the frame, allowing it to drape itself down on the sides (see Fig. 12).

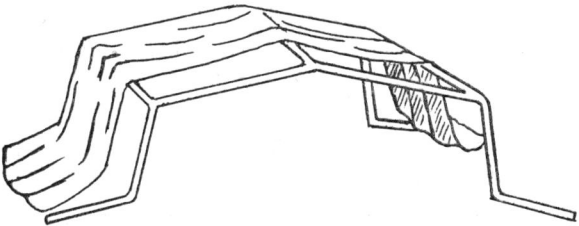

Fig. 12

As a rule, a frame tent is pitched with its back to the wind, and should it have to be pitched in windy conditions it pays to peg out at once the two main guy ropes which come from the top corners of the tent (this stops the tent blowing away). This is done while the remainder of the party hang on to the fabric.

Now raise the tent to its full height, using the same method as for raising it to its knees. If it is windy, peg down the remainder of the main guys immediately and, if necessary, insert some of the pegs to hold the bottom of the fabric. You may have to move these later, but at this stage they are only used to prevent wind damage. Go inside the tent and, having closed the zips, tie up all the tapes which position the fabric on the frame. Still from the inside, adjust the legs of the frame if necessary; this is done by lifting each leg and allowing it to return to the ground in its natural position.

Now, from the outside, making sure that all the zips are still fully closed, peg down the corners. It is important that these pegs are correctly placed, as incorrect pegging down can put undue stress on the fabric and cause permanent damage. Personally, I like to insert the pegs on either side of the doorway, making sure that the fabric is taut, as this prevents flapping in the wind which can cause damage. Try to make sure that the doorway will zip all the way down to the bottom. It is very easy to misplace these pegs at each side of the entrance so that there is too great a stress on the zips; this not only strains the zips themselves, causing undue wear, but also prevents them from closing to the bottom – especially when the tent is damp – thus causing a draught in the tent and straining the zips and fabric. I am sorry if this sounds very complicated, but do not worry too much. After erecting the tent a few times, you will see what I mean and soon put it up quickly and correctly.

Take the inner tent inside the main structure and spread it out on the groundsheet, making sure that the doors face the living part of the tent. This may sound obvious, but it is very easy to erect the inner tent only to find that the doors are facing the back of the main tent so that you cannot get in. Funny but very annoying! We always put a sheet of plastic between the groundsheet and the ground; this prevents the groundsheet from getting wet and muddy, which is a great advantage when you want to break camp. Peg down the groundsheet, putting the pegs through the loops or rings which are positioned all around it. Now hang the inner tent in position by attaching the rubber loops and hooks supplied to the main frame. If you hang up the inner tent before pegging down the groundsheet, you will not be able to get at the loops supplied for the pegs without pushing against the fabric of the main tent and straining it. This can be done from outside, but it is a nuisance and you can damage the fabric with your mallet.

The next step is to erect the awning which, in most cases, consists of nothing more than pushing two spikes through the holes provided at each corner of the awning followed by the placing of the pegs, usually two to each corner, or the simple extension of the roof frame (see Fig. 13).

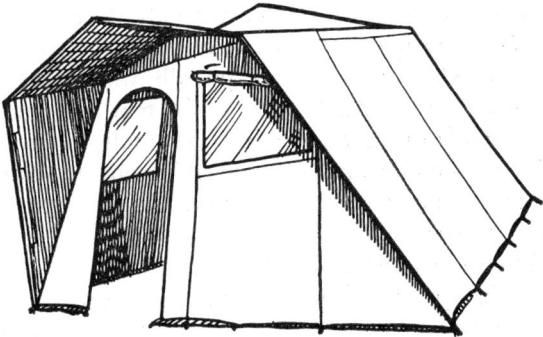

Fig. 13

The final item is the simple erection of the small awning over the window, after which the tent should be standing without any wrinkles in the fabric. However, you cannot expect perfection if you have to pitch on uneven ground.

To dismantle a frame tent the erection procedure is followed in reverse; but there are a few snags, such as having to break camp in wet or windy weather, and, as clumsy dismantling just as much as clumsy erection can cause damage and build up trouble for the future, I will run through the procedure. The dismantling of all types of tents follows much the same principles, but, in view of its comparatively high cost, particular attention must be paid in the case of a frame tent.

The first step is to go inside and check that the pockets in the sleeping compartments are empty and sweep the groundsheet clean; then zip up the inner tent doors completely. At this stage you can unhook the inner tent from the main frame and allow the fabric to fall upon the groundsheet, at once tidying it ready to fold up. Incidentally, while this is going on another member of the party goes round removing all the pegs from both the inner and main tent – unless, of course, it is windy. Use a spare peg or peg-puller, which only costs 5p or so, to remove the pegs. Never pull on the cords, rubber loops or walls of the tent.

With the inner tent neatly folded on the groundsheet, fold the latter over so that the underside is outside and wipe any mud or moisture from it. Now the groundsheet can be folded or rolled longways, the mud or moisture again being wiped off as this job proceeds. The inner tent has to be folded tightly if it is to go inside the main tent and pack into its bag. I divide my tent into four bags, containing respectively the main tent, the inner tent, main tent poles, and the poles of the window and main awnings. This makes packing the tent a simple job and also allows easier handling when the tent is moved to the next site or taken home.

Having disposed of the inner tent, we now start on the outer. First, walk round the tent and remove all dirt and grit from the walls and the plastic skirting. Undo the tapes which hold the fabric to the frame at all the corners and throw the awning back onto the top of the tent. Now lower the frame to its knees. It is important to throw as much of the fabric of the main tent as possible up onto the top of the frame before you lower it to half-height. This has two advantages: it keeps the fabric off the ground should it be wet or muddy, and avoids the possibility of the material getting trapped between the frame sections and torn as the frame is lowered. It also prevents the fabric from being walked on, although this should never be allowed to happen. In a high wind, of course, it is unwise to unpeg the tent until it is lowered to its knees, and then you should always unpeg the leeward side first and dismantle the tent from that side where it cannot be caught by the wind; it is essential to keep it down and pegged, at least at the corners, until the frame is on its knees. Never undo the windward pegs unless you are sure you have full control of the fabric.

Let us assume, however, that the weather is fine: the fabric has been thrown up onto the top of the frame, which now has to be lowered to half-height. To avoid strain upon the frame it is better to have two people available. Lift the two legs at one end simultaneously and pull apart the joint which joins the two halves of the leg tubes; then lower the frame to half-height, the lower halves of the tube now being flat on the ground. If, like me, you have a six-leg tent, it is a good idea to remove the middle legs as the first step. I do this because they generally fall out by themselves as you lift the end of the frame, or if they remain in position they do not allow the end of the frame where you have broken the legs to be lowered to the ground. The main object must be to avoid straining the frame. Anyway, finally lower the pair of legs at the second end to half-height.

Having got the frame to its knees, I replace the middle legs at half-height to support the centre whilst I am folding the fabric, which now has to be tidied up. Tidy the awning first, pulling it back across the roof, and then fold the canvas towards the centre of the frame. Take care that the zip does not get caught in the fabric anywhere because this can easily break threads. It does not matter whether you fold it lengthways, i.e. from the front to the back of the tent, or from the sides. I always fold it from the front, folding the front of the fabric back over the awning to the middle of the roof, and then fold from the back, again taking the fabric to the middle. This is the time to get the bag which is to hold the fabric and measure it against the partly folded tent. When you have an idea of how long your final fold must be, fold the fabric, first from the front towards the centre and then from the back, arranging things so that you have it just the right size to fit the bag. The rest of the job is easy; the folding is repeated, taking each end in turn towards the centre, and the folded fabric is then moved to the ground, where it can be rolled up and placed in the bag. When you lower the fabric to the ground, it pays to put it on a sheet of plastic or newspaper to keep it clean. Many of these jobs can be done at the same time. How they are arranged depends on the number of people available.

Having disposed of the fabric, remove the legs from the roof frame, taking them out a pair at a time, and place them in the appropriate bag. Now all you have left is the roof section. As this is all spring linked together, you must find a method of packing it away, bearing in mind the very important point that you need to erect the tent without difficulties at a later date.

My method, which may sound very difficult, will be found to be quite easy when you attempt it in practice. Working with three people if possible (I think two are essential if you are not to place undue strain on the spring links), start at the long side and fold back the frame to the centre. We do exactly the same at the other side until we are left with the frame reduced to the width of one unit or pole of the frame. We then repeat the procedure, starting at one end and then the other, until finally the roof section is folded so that it will fit into its sack.

4 *The Tentomatic Tent*

There is one other type of tent suitable for the car camper; in fact, it is designed as a major accessory of the car and can be only used by the camper who drives onto the site – this is the Tentomatic. Since the frame tent became popular, there were no major innovations in camping, with the exception of the recent increase in popularity of the trailer tent and motor caravan, until the introduction of this tent. It has a semi-automatic frame which forms the roof rack of the vehicle – a roof rack on which it is also possible to pack normal baggage. The tent compares favourably with the standard frame tent of similar size, being large enough for four or five people. Its weight is 120 lbs and the cost a little more than the standard frame tent. The roof rack looks very much like the usual type and

Fig. 14

is very strong, clipping to the roof guttering (see Fig. 14). Fittings can be supplied for all cars. The tent fabric fits onto the roof rack, and the legs and pegs are supplied in a separate bag. This bag and other camping gear can be placed on the roof rack on top of the tent material, subject to a safe weight for your vehicle.

To erect the tent drive the car onto the spot selected for your site. Before you pay for your pitch, it is worth checking that you can drive your car to it. You can in most cases, but very occasionally you find a site which has a separate car park. If you cannot take your car to the pitch to load and unload, this is not the site for a Tentomatic owner – so move on to another.

Having taken your car to the selected pitch, you must first unload all your luggage, and the bag containing the tent legs and pegs, from the roof rack; then you can start to put up the tent. By pressing buttons on the roof rack, extensions spring out. To these you fix the legs, which are colour coded for convenience. Next the side rails are placed in position (Fig. 15 shows this stage) and the canvas unfolded and drawn out to the corners of the frame where

Fig. 15

Fig. 16

it is tied (see Fig. 16). Now the roof rack clips are released and the legs extended to a height sufficient for you to be able to drive the car away. The tent is unfolded over the frame and the legs are raised to their full height. Finally, peg out the material. The tent contains an inner tent divided into two sleeping compartments and fitted with a sewn-in groundsheet; there is also a small awning (see Fig. 13).

What I like about this tent is the strength of the legs,

which are telescopic, allowing you to adjust the frame on uneven ground. You have to peg down the fabric tight, otherwise the weight of the roof rack tends to make the tent sway in the wind. It is in no danger of coming down, but is just a little disconcerting at first. I do not think this tent is much quicker to erect than a frame tent if you take the time from stopping the car to the time the last peg is in, but it is so much easier and the heavy material does not have to be humped up into place. The tent can easily be erected by one person, which is not very practical in the case of a standard frame tent.

When breaking camp, the tent is outstanding. You drive the car under the fabric instead of lifting it up, and it goes away almost as easily wet as when dry – the fabric must, of course, be allowed to dry out as soon as possible.

Special notes for campers

With particular reference to those camping for the first time with a frame tent

During certain humid weather conditions and when there is heavy dew in the early morning, it is inevitable that condensation will form on the inside of the canvas and also on the tubular work of frame tents. (Sometimes mistaken as not waterproofed cloth.) To clear this, ample ventilation is recommended.

The cloth from which camping tents are made breathes, and if a cloth was used which did not breathe (i.e. cloth proofed with rubber or P.V.C.), whilst giving better waterproofing qualities than the normal cloths, the non-breathing cloth would not be suitable on account of the condensation problems.

Sometimes when sudden heavy rain starts, there may be slight spraying from the canvas, but this will, after a short time, cease when the fabric has had the opportunity of tightening up by swelling of the fibres of the cloth.

Shrinkage. Some shrinkage of tent cloths takes place on becoming wet, but this is normal and is adjusted by the rubber fastenings and recovers after drying out.

When a tent is dismantled in very wet conditions, shrinkage that has taken place may not be regained. To overcome this re-erect tent as soon as possible under tension.

Spring Linkage of Frame Tent Parts. The object of spring linking the parts is to facilitate the quick erection of tents so that the parts do not have to be sorted out before erection. However, unless care is used, it is possible that the springs can become over-strained and sometimes break. Nevertheless, this does not preclude the building up of the frame.

It is recommended, therefore, that care is taken that the spring joints are not over-strained.

Some users discard the springs and make their own identifications on the tubes to facilitate erection.

(*Supplied by Hawleys of Walsall, manufacturers of Goodall tents.*)

Chapter 5

The Trailer Tent

Although the occasional tent built on a trailer has been seen at camping sites for a long time – these were usually home built – it is only recently that the trailer tent has become very popular. There can be no doubt that this form of camping has come to stay in a big way.

What are the advantages of this type of tent? It is towed and therefore does not overload the car. It takes less time to erect than the conventional tent – in fact, it can be put up by one person in a matter of minutes (Figs. 17 to 21

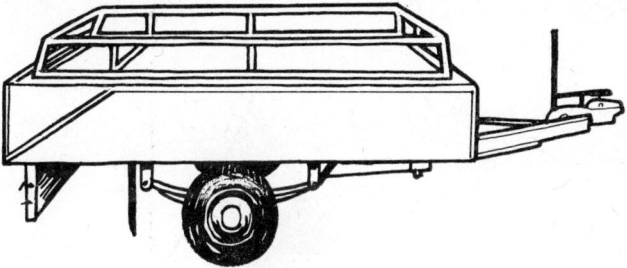

Fig. 17

show the erection process). The trailer tent provides off-the-ground living, which makes for warmth and comfort (see Figs. 22 and 23). It is much lighter than a caravan and can be towed comfortably by the smallest car. The rear window provides full rear-view vision, so there is no need for such aids as a periscope or extended wing mirrors.

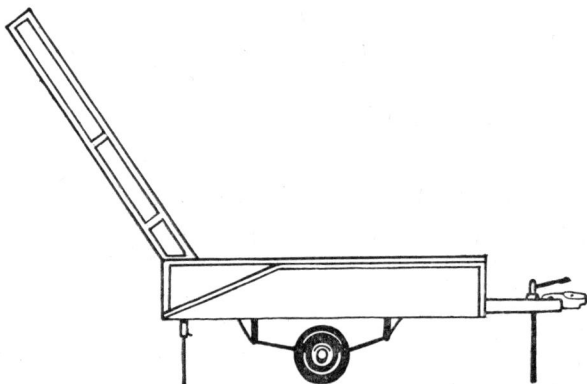

Fig. 18

Fig. 19

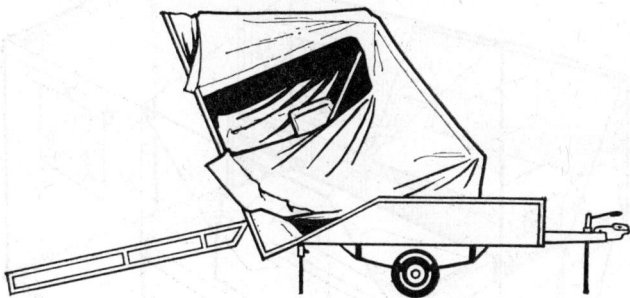

Fig. 20

Fig. 21

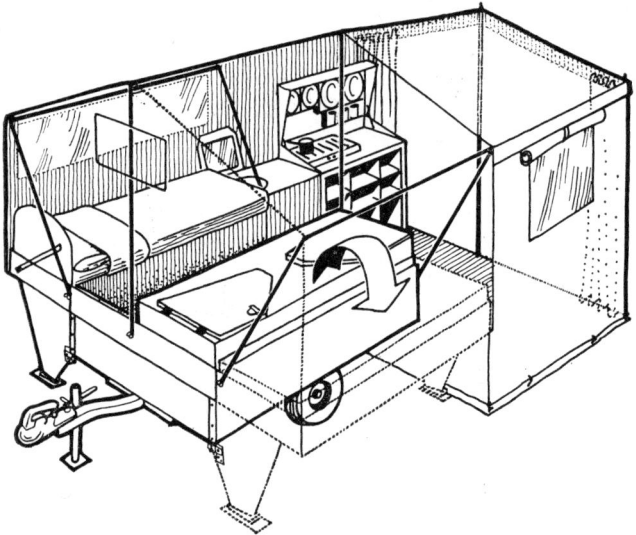

Fig. 22

Now let us look at the disadvantages. When it is not in use, you have to find a space to park your trailer tent. You have the problem of reversing and in the United Kingdom are restricted to a speed limit of 40 miles per hour. But the main drawback is the price. This type of tent is expensive when all the necessary extras, such as mattresses, have been purchased, and if you buy an awning as well it can exceed the cost of the popular makes of caravan. I think it is rather ridiculous to pay between £300 and £400 for a trailer tent when you can buy a good caravan for less. It is possible, however, to buy some trailer tents in kit form. Being considerably cheaper, these kits bring the trailer tent more into line with the cost of a standard frame tent plus a luggage trailer.

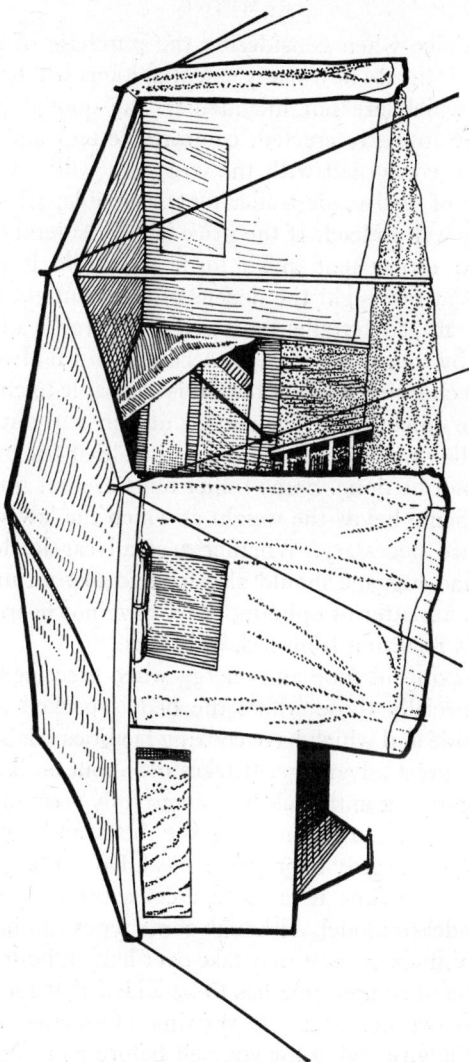

Fig. 23

My advice when considering the purchase of a trailer tent is to estimate how many essential items will have to be bought which are not included in the quoted price. If you want an easily erected, comfortable tent and are not too much concerned with the cost, you will find a large selection of well-made trailer tents available, all of which tow very well indeed. If the price is a consideration, then buy your trailer tent in kit form and build it yourself. Whereas at first sight the dozens of pieces might frighten you to death, such trailer tents as the "Mirror" can, in fact, be built by someone with no special skill in woodworking.

When choosing a trailer tent, it is advisable to check that it can be erected and dismantled in rain without getting the bedding wet – I am told that with at least one make this just cannot be done. Some trailer tents are not fitted with brakes, being below the weight at which the law says that brakes are necessary. Whether a small car loaded with people and luggage should also have to tow an unbraked trailer is a matter of opinion, but I have not heard of any accidents resulting from lack of brakes.

The saving in time and energy when erecting a trailer tent, especially those where the bed is packed away already made and which have cooking facilities readily available, is a great advantage. It takes me about an hour from stopping my car at the selected site to fully erect my Raclet frame tent, including making the beds and unpacking crockery, etc., ready to prepare a meal. Do not forget, however, that the time it takes to erect a trailer tent varies from model to model. Although some types can be put up in five minutes or so, it may take over half an hour to erect others – and to this time has to be added that required to erect the awning, if any. As the time of erection varies so much, I advise trying for yourself before you buy.

One point to bear in mind is that there have been occasions where site wardens have refused to accept trailer tents as tents and the unfortunate owners have then found that they are not accepted as caravanners either. This should not deter you as these cases are rare, and I mention them only because they occasioned some publicity in the camping press at the time. The Camping Club of Great Britain and Ireland accept trailer tents as tents on their sites, and so do most other site owners.

To sum up, if you want really comfortable camping with little trouble in erecting and dismantling your tent, a trailer tent is the mobile home for you, especially if you can afford a fully-fitted trailer or are willing and able to assemble your own outfit from a kit. Your only problems are the speed limit and the difficulty of reversing.

Chapter 6

Main Items of Equipment : Beds and Bedding; Camp Furniture; Portable Sanitation

The selection of the equipment you will require in addition to your tent is quite a problem. Somehow you have to strike a balance between luxury and the limitations imposed by your transport facilities. However, I can see no reason to despise comfort just because you are camping, especially if you have your wife and family with you.

The main activities in your tent are sleeping and eating. No matter how their personal tastes differ, all campers have to sleep and eat. Let us first have a look at the sleeping side.

Beds and Bedding

Comfort and warmth are essential, so unless you are a super-lightweight type forget about using the ground or bracken as a bed, although the latter can be surprisingly warm and comfortable. What choice of beds is available?

Beds
Your main choice is between the camp bed and the inflatable mattress. The camp bed is cheaper and raises you off the ground. It is long-lasting and, most important, folds into a reasonably small space. It is more substantial than many makes of air bed and, of course, is heavier. As cold

air gets under the camp bed, you will require a blanket or
something similar beneath you on cold nights; the air bed,
on the other hand, insulates you from the ground. The old-
fashioned wooden frame officer-type bed is seldom seen
nowadays; it was far too heavy to last in these days of
lightweight camping kit. The comparatively light metal
framed beds vary in colour and style. You can buy the

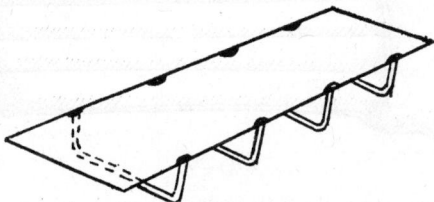

Fig. 24

straightforward safari bed (see Fig. 24) or obtain a type
fitted with ratchets which doubles as a chair during the
day (see Fig. 25). The latter is rather expensive, however,

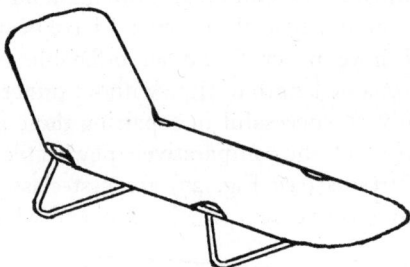

Fig. 25

and takes up more space. Before spending the extra money,
consider the transport problem and whether the cost will
be balanced by a reasonable amount of use; if you do

decide on the ratchet type, be sure to try it out before purchasing.

Inflatable beds (see Fig. 26) are very comfortable if blown up to the correct pressure. Too soft, they are naturally uncomfortable, but when too hard there is tendency

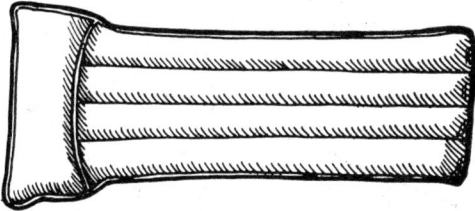

Fig. 26

for the sleeper to roll off the edge; they should be just hard enough to mould themselves to the body. After a few nights' use, however, you learn to get the pressure exactly right. As I have indicated, the air bed is warmer than the camp type by virtue of the air trapped inside it which insulates you from the ground and the night air which can attack you from underneath. Perhaps I have been unfortunate, but I have never found an inflatable bed which lasted a reasonable length of time without puncturing, nor have I been very successful in repairing these punctures. On the other hand, the comparatively new waffle construction air mattresses (see Fig. 27) are first-class. Deflated, they fold into a convenient small space, and when inflated

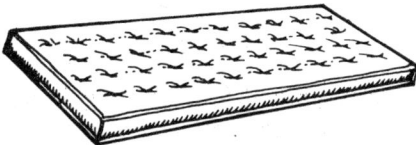

Fig. 27

look like a conventional internally sprung mattress and are just about as comfortable. As yet, I am unable to say from personal experience how long they will last, but I think they will prove very good value for money.

The battle between the camp bed and the air bed enthusiasts has been going on for several years. In the past I have always been a camp bed supporter, but I think the future will find me the confirmed "waffle" man. Providing they are treated with care so that they do not puncture, the air beds are lighter and do not take up as much room on the journey as the camp beds. They neither have odd legs sticking out to disconnect electric cables in your car boot, not do they damage the groundsheet, which camp beds can do if not carefully handled. I think a beginner is probably better off with an air bed, but do get a good one that will last and take care of it.

There is another alternative – the rubber mattress (see Fig. 28). Made of soft rubber, it is merely laid on the

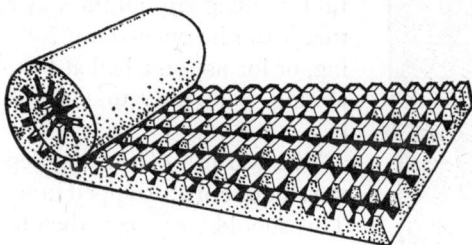

Fig. 28

ground. It will provide a reasonable night's sleep, but in my opinion is not as comfortable as the other types, nor does it pack away into such a small space. If space is no object, however, it gives real comfort if used on top of a frame camp bed.

If you are a lightweight camper, the rubber mattress and camp bed are out; they take up too much space and are too heavy to carry. The best bet in this case is the hip-length air bed, which is light, can be inflated by mouth and takes up very little of your valuable packing space.

Sleeping Bags

These vary considerably in both price and warmth. You can buy sleeping bags at prices from £2·50 to over £30. These are extremes, of course, and no one would dream of advising the family camper to buy an expensive specialist bag designed for high-altitude sub-zero conditions such as that shown in Fig. 29. The family camper needs a bag which will be warm, hard-wearing and will look nice. In addition it must be large enough to turn over in without turning the bag over as well (see Fig. 30). It is also useful if the bag zips all the way round so that it can be opened out fully for airing, or for use on a bed at home, or for joining to another to make a double bag.

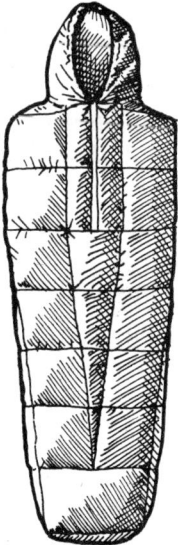

The warmth of the bag depends on the amount of air trapped in the filling. This should compress when the bag is rolled up for transporting and expand when it is opened out for sleeping. The best filling in this respect is down. Terylene is almost as warm, but does not compress quite as much.

Fig. 29

In recent years, campers have realised the value of the dual-purpose bag, which is hard-wearing, warm and light,

Fig. 30

and bright and cheerful. The cover is usually nylon, whilst the packing can be terylene, courtelle, acrilan or orlon. These fibres are all well known and are first-class for filling sleeping bags, being soft, warm and resilient – requirements as important as their being resistant to insects and damp.

Modern bags with synthetic fillings have a high warmth-to-weight ratio. They act like insulators, keeping you warm when the weather is cold and cool when it is hot. The packing does not bunch up like the old-fashioned kapok, thus leaving cold patches, and the bag fully regains its original softness when shaken out. A good filling below you does not pack down flat. This is important since the cold strikes just as much from below as it does from above. The bags are stitched to keep the filling in place, but remember that there is no filling where there are seams and that the absence of filling allows heat to escape on cold nights.

Bags with synthetic filling can be washed without too much difficulty. A down-filled bag, however, must be dry cleaned, so before attempting to wash your bag make certain that you know what type of filling it has.

A synthetic fibre-filled bag does not roll up so compactly as a down-filled bag, but with care it can still be rolled into quite a small bundle. In some cases a cloth bag is provided, often made in the same attractive material as the sleeping bag itself. Some manufacturers provide a plastic bag which soon tears, but if you purchase your sleeping bag from a supplier who hires out camping kit ask for one of the containers they use for hire sleeping bags. These are made to correct size and are strong; most dealers will sell you one very cheaply. You can obtain inner sheets which are said to prolong the life of a bag; certainly they protect the inside of the bag from being soiled. Take great care of your sleeping bag – as a rule, a repair can cost as much as or even more than a new bag.

When the time comes to choose a bag it is important to select one of the correct size, and to do this it is not sufficient to see the bags rolled up neatly in their colourful containers. Most suppliers display their stock on hangers to enable you to see the length and width. You can obtain a bag varying in size from "king-size" to mini-bags for children. If you are a sixteen-stone six-footer, get a "king-size" bag, but it will be far too large for the child or average-sized woman. Even the shape varies from that shown in Fig. 30 to the type illustrated in Fig. 31.

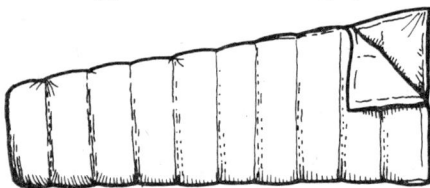

Fig. 31

I do not wish to give the impression you should not buy a down-filled bag – a good bag of this type is wonderful. It is warm and cosy and very light, and packs into an extremely small space. A good one is tremendously expensive, but if you can afford it you will have many warm and comfortable nights. Do make sure, however, that you cannot feel too many hard stalks – this indicates an excess of large feathers in the mixture.

Camp Furniture

Here we have to consider the equipment needed for the other main activity in your tent – eating. I shall discuss the various types of cookers available, together with methods of heating and lighting in camp, in the following chapter. But this leaves quite a few important items connected with the eating side: cooking utensils, crockery, cutlery, kitchen units, tables and chairs.

Cooking Utensils

What you buy must depend on your facilities for carrying it. You can take quite a big double-burner stove if you are travelling by car, but are restricted to a small lightweight article should you be on foot. There are some very nice small pressure stoves on the market which, together with a non-stick frying pan, will provide almost unlimited variation in your food. Alternatively, you can buy a combination set of pans with lids, all of

Fig. 32

which fit neatly into each other (see Figs. 32 and 33).

The drawback with the pressure cooker is the space it takes up and its weight. Although mini-models are avail-

able, they are still rather bulky and heavy, weighing about
2½ lbs. However, I was very impressed with one particular

Fig. 33

model which looked like
a saucepan with a safety
lug and locking lugs,
but cooked at an inside
temperature of 121° C
(250° F) at 15 lbs pres-
sure. This was camp
cooking at its most effi-
cient. Non-stick pans
are a godsend – they
save greasy washing up
and are easy to serve
from.

The combination sets of pans have been in use for years.
The pans are used for boiling, whilst the lids, which have
handles, double as frying pans. Care must be taken when
frying to avoid burning the food as the lids are made of
thin metal, and you may find it difficult to remove food
from the pan with a serving slice because of the height
of the sides of this type of utensil.

For boiling water, you can buy a camp kettle quite
cheaply (made of thin metal to allow quick boiling), These
kettles are of the lidless variety and are filled through their
spouts which have screw-on caps. The latter allow the
kettle to be used as a water container or carrier, but on no
account should the kettle be heated without first removing
its spout cover.

Crockery and Cutlery
As is the case with all camping equipment, there is a large
selection of suitable crockery and cutlery on the market.

Nowadays, it is possible to obtain sets of plastic plates, cups and saucers in a variety of attractive colours and patterns which, according to the manufacturers, do not discolour or give the food or drink the unpleasant flavour so traditional in plastic. I have not experimented with these myself. As far as "eating irons" are concerned, there are the camping sets consisting of knife, fork and spoon (and sometimes teaspoon) which either clip together or fit in neat plastic cases. These are usually cheap, but often not of very high quality. However, they are quite satisfactory and children seem to like them.

Picnic sets containing both crockery and cutlery are on sale in the shops, ranging from the most expensive, packed in elaborate cases and containing thermos flasks and condiment containers, to those packed in cardboard boxes. Generally, the more you spend, the better the quality. The snag with the set is that you always get items which you do not need, or possess already, and the containers take up too much space. We always take our everyday crockery and cutlery packed in a plastic bucket. We seldom break the china – in fact, I cannot remember ever having done so – and we do not lose the cutlery. The plastic bucket fits into any odd space in the car boot and doubles for washing up, and washing clothes and ourselves.

Kitchen Units and Cooking Tables

There are two requirements for safe and comfortable cooking: a firm base and the correct height. If you travel with a caravan or camping trailer which has a built-in kitchen unit, the first requirement will not concern you as the vehicle is necessarily steady when you pitch. It is not easy to alter the height of the built-in cooker, but you should have considered this point when buying your caravan or trailer tent. In a tent, however, the situation is different. You have bought a tent, which means you are on the ground to start with. If you wish to raise the height of your cooker, you will have to provide a table, and that table must be steady on the ground. There are many types of tables about, most of which fold flat and take up very little space, yet providing a working surface and shelves when erected.

What are we looking for in a working table? In my opinion there are four essential requirements. These are:

1. Height.
2. Steadiness on the ground.
3. Security for the cooker and utensils on the table.
4. Protection against the wind.

Let us have a look at these one at a time.

1 *Height.* Exactly what is the correct height is a matter of opinion, but as there is little choice in this respect no doubt you will have to put up with the height of the cooking table available which suits you in other respects.

2 *Steadiness on the ground.* This is vital – it is not safe to use a table which is unsteady. Naturally, if you select a well-made table and site it on level ground, there is no problem; it will stand firm and solid. However, my experience of camping sites is that ground which appears level and smooth when you pitch on it reveals a surprising number of lumps and hollows when you come to set up your camp furniture.

Manufacturers produce tables with three types of legs. The most common is that which has four ordinary legs (see Fig. 34), but many have legs which are joined together at each end (see Fig. 35). The snag with these is that any

Fig. 34

Fig. 35

rise in the ground between the legs causes the table to rock. The third type of table has separate legs, all of which are telescopic and adjust in height. So far, I have not come across an actual cooking table with telescopic legs, but they may exist. If you cannot find one, you can obtain an ordinary camp table with this type of leg and use it for cooking if it is otherwise suitable. This means, however, that you will not have the useful shelves which are part of most specialist cooking tables.

3 *Security for the cooker and utensils on the table*. This is very much linked up with the steadiness of the table on the ground. Given the steadiest of tables, however, if its surface is the wrong size and shape, and of unsuitable material, the table will be dangerous, for the slightest knock will unload the boiling contents on the ground or, even worse, on to you or a member of your family.

Carelessly planned cooking can be dangerous in camp. The best and safest tables incorporate the gas jets as an integral part of the outfit. But if you buy a table when you already have your cooker, do not merely stick the cooker on the table and get cracking on your meal – make sure it is well balanced and cannot slide off the edge – for example,

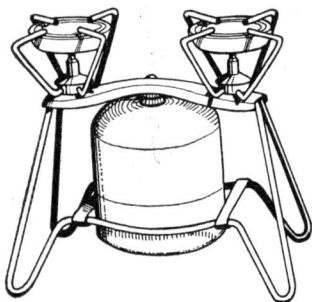

the Camping Gaz Standard Double-Burner Cooker shown in Fig. 36 will almost certainly slip if placed on a narrow metal table and may cause an accident. It may be worth taking the top of the cooker off the gas cylinder, fixing it securely to the table and feeding it to the cylinder by suitable tubing. The snag here is that such

Fig. 36

alterations make it difficult or even impossible to fold the table flat.

4 *Protection against the wind*. No matter how much heat your cooker produces your food will take ages to cook if it is working in a cooling wind. This is not only very annoying

to hungry campers but also extravagant on the fuel. It is essential, therefore, to protect your cooker from the wind and, as far as possible, from cold air. The easy way out, of course, is to cook inside, but unless you have a kitchen unit which has some device for protecting the tent wall from splashing fat and food this can cause damage. An alternative is to rig up a canvas screen as a windbreak. Those sold as suntraps are very suitable for this purpose, or you can obtain or make a screen to match your tent. The disadvantage with these screens is that they are bulky, and you may not have room to carry one.

Some cooking tables are supplied with a screen which fits onto the end and one side of the table, and thus protects the cooker on two or three sides (see Fig. 37).

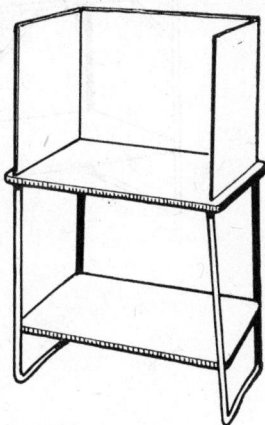

Fig. 37

This works fairly well if your cooker lies flat on the table, but if it stands high on the top of a gas cylinder the flame will be unprotected and, in this case, an additional screen will be required if you are to cook in the open air. The table shown in Fig. 37 folds up into a small case (see Fig. 38).

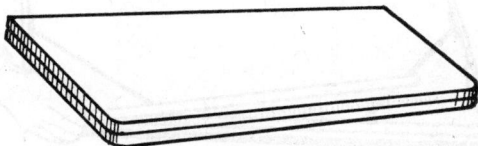

Fig. 38

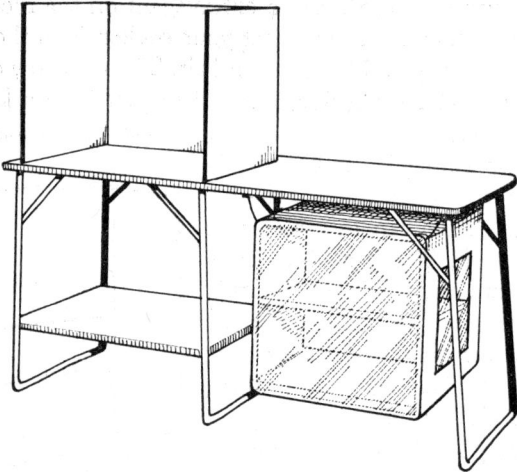

Fig. 39

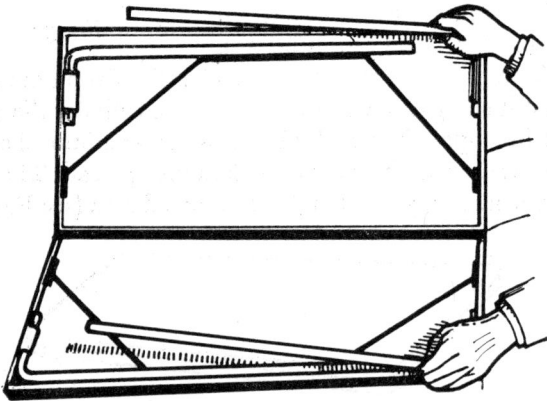

Fig. 40

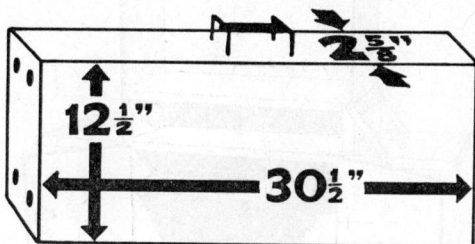

Fig. 41

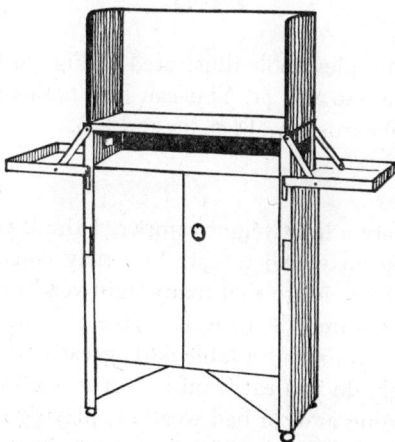

Fig. 42

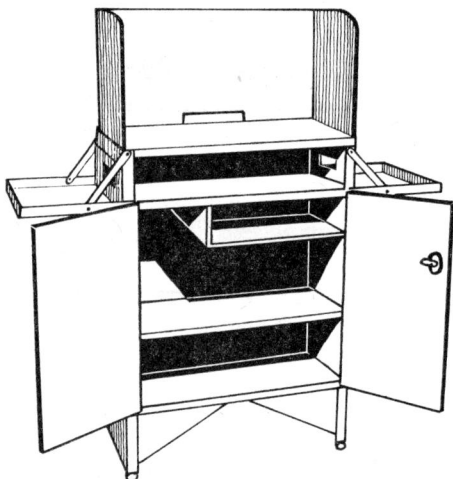

Fig. 43

The more complex table illustrated in Fig. 39 folds up as
shown in Figs. 40 and 41. You can buy tables which also
serve as cupboards (see Figs. 42 and 43).

Eating Tables
Unless you are a lightweight camper, I think you will require a table on which to eat. You may consider this a
luxury and I am aware that many lightweight enthusiasts
happily settle round their meals on the ground, but if you
have room in your tent a table adds greatly to your comfort. Not only do you eat from it, but it is also useful for
writing, reading and, in bad weather, playing cards. Like
cooking tables, "eating" tables fold flat and can be obtained with the various types of legs. Obviously, they must
stand steady, and I find that the tables which are made

with each pair of legs formed like a continuous tube (see Fig. 35, page 61) tend to rock. On the other hand, four individual legs (see Fig. 34, page 61) tend to make holes in the groundsheet should you use one in the living section. I have already mentioned the table which has independent telescopic legs, enabling it to be levelled up and steadied on rough ground. This is good, although it tends

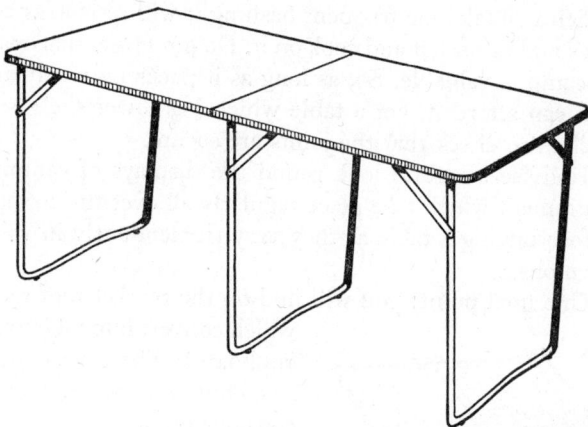

Fig. 44

to be expensive. If you have a table with individual legs, you can buy or make flat ends which fit onto them and prevent damage to the groundsheet. Unless, however, you have very sharp-ended legs on your table and put considerable weight on it, you are unlikely to tear the groundsheet if you take care (the real danger to the groundsheet is your chairs).

The simple folding table which folds flat can be packed away at the bottom of your roof rack or car boot. I tie mine against the back of the front seat of the car and in this way it takes up little space, but perhaps I am lucky in that I have plenty of leg space in the back of my car. You can purchase double-length tables with several pairs of legs (see Fig. 44) which can be used for cooking, preparing food and eating. Once a table is up, its shape does not matter much, but what is important is whether you can pack it in your car. Get a strong model with a good top which will take the frequent bashing it will receive as you pack and unpack it and cook on it. Do not forget that space in camp is valuable. So, as long as it packs up nicely and you can afford it, get a table which has lower shelves as well. Also check that the joints are secure.

I advise a careful look round the displays of camping equipment which take place regularly all over the country before buying a table as they vary tremendously in value for money.

One final point: you will find on the market roof racks which convert into tables and cupboards. These are expensive, but you might like to consider them.

Fig. 45

Chairs

No matter how active you are the time will come when you will want to sit down, if only to eat. Most of us like to be able to sit down in comfort at odd times during the day. Personally, I sit to shave first thing in the morning, for meals, to read the paper and to write or read in the evening. Thus to me a comfortable

chairs are the essentials. Chairs come in all shapes,
... and comfort of no great moment ...

Fig. 46

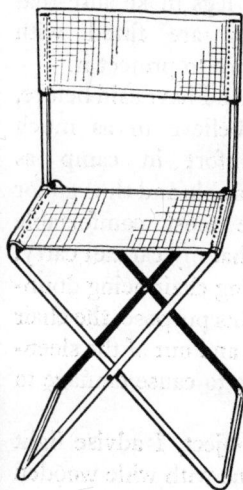

Fig. 47

chair is one of the essentials. Chairs come in all shapes, sizes, colours and prices, and consist of material mounted onto a metal or wooden frame.

The selection varies from the simple wooden stool shown in Fig. 45 to the complicated wonder illustrated in Fig. 46, which doubles, or rather trebles, as a chair, reclining couch and bed. You can have simple chairs (see Fig. 47), chairs with arm rests (see Fig. 48), padding or springs. Most chairs have the "U" shaped type of legs which save the ground-sheet from damage (see Fig. 48), but if you decide on a chair which has independent tubular legs make sure that they are fitted with shoes to protect it.

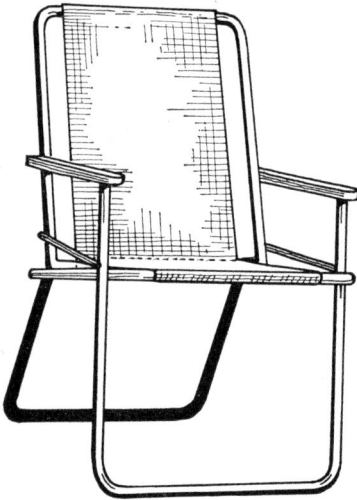

Fig. 48

As I have said before, I believe in as much comfort in camp as possible and thus go for the most comfortable beds and chairs that I can afford or that my car can carry. But I do not really like to see a reclining chair being doubled as a bed. Even if it is suitable for this purpose, the chair is usually bulky, and pulling a bed in and out of the sleeping compartment twice a day is liable to cause damage to the tent unless great care is taken.

Unless space and weight are no object, I advise light metal folding chairs. If you can get one with wide wooden arms (see Fig. 48), I think you have the best type. On the other hand, if you use a reclining chair in the garden at home, it is ridiculous not to make use of it in camp should it be suitable. I take two folding chairs for my wife and myself, and two folding stools for the boys.

Most chairs and stools use canvas material of all sorts of colours and patterns. Despite the introduction of the many new fibres, canvas has retained its popularity for this purpose and it is my experience that the man-made fibres tear away from the tacks or other fixing.

Do not forget to check the joints. They should be amply strong and firm; also ensure that there is plenty of material where it is joined to the frame. It can be very annoying when the canvas pulls away from the chair on the first occasion you sit down. This has happened to me in an otherwise strong and comfortable chair.

Water Containers

These are essential. Many types are available – of all shapes and sizes – with and without taps. I always use a simple, 2–gallon polythene type (see Fig. 49) which looks like a small jerrycan. It is not too heavy to handle when full and does not take up too much space. Poly-

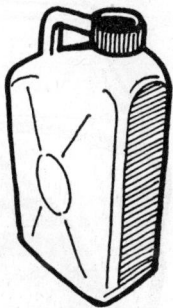

Fig. 49

thene containers tend to discolour inside if not rinsed out regularly. Should this happen, you can clean them by filling them with a solution of washing soda in hot water and allowing it to stand for a few days; then rinse out thoroughly with plenty of clean water. If the stains are really stubborn, use the old army method of washing up – sand. Half fill the container with water and gritty sand and shake hard.

Cool Containers and Refrigerators

Although these are more for the caravanner or the car camper with a large carrying capacity, storing food in camp is important, as stale or bad food will result in an upset tummy. The food problem has two obvious solutions: either you buy what is required for the immediate meal and eat it with little delay, or you buy several days' supply and pack the left-overs neatly and safely in covered containers. Safely? Your butter will become a soft mush and bacteria will breed happily – the result? – a spoilt holiday. We always carry a small reserve supply of tinned foods, unopened of course, sufficient merely to last over a weekend or for a day when shopping is inconvenient. Unsealed foods, such as meat, we buy in just sufficient quantity for the coming meal.

You can obtain a collapsible larder made of fabric with hardboard shelves and a netting front which allows air to circulate (see Fig. 50). This folds flat, and provides quite a lot of space when hung from a hook on the tent frame.

Fig. 50

More ambitious is the vacuum flask store. Here you have vacuum containers of various sizes. Food put in hot remains hot, whilst cold food stays cold.

Most expensive and ambitious of all is the ice-box (see Fig. 51). As a rule, these are straightforward boxes insulated with glass fibre. They are bright, rustproof and rigid. In Europe ice is usually obtainable at camp sites, fishmongers or butchers.

A development of the ice-box is the container insulated with plastic foam. This works because air is a first-class insulator and, as the plastic foam consists to a great extent of air trapped in the material,

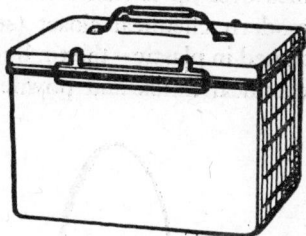

Fig. 51

the result is an insulated box. If you put cool food in such a box it will remain cool. Ice can be put in as well to reduce the temperature. Gas or electrically operated refrigerators are often fitted in motor caravans.

There are a large number of containers on the market using various systems of keeping food cool. It would be well worth your while to browse around an exhibition before you decide to buy.

Portable Sanitation

I am one of those people who constantly press for better camping sites, and in my opinion a clean and well-equipped sanitation block is the first, and possibly only, essential for a site. Many campers, however, do not agree with me; they prefer what is known as "wild camping". The camping clubs are inclined to hold their weekend rendezvous in a beautiful spot where the sanitation is nil, and "provide your own sanitation" is not an unusual phrase to appear on the information leaflet.

The old custom of digging holes or trenches was efficient, but in these days of family camping it is no longer acceptable. There is a demand for something which measures up to home conditions. There is an answer – a modern chemical closet (see Fig. 52). This is well designed in plastic – the tin bucket is a thing of the past – and chemical fluids and powders kill the unpleasant smells.

Fig. 52

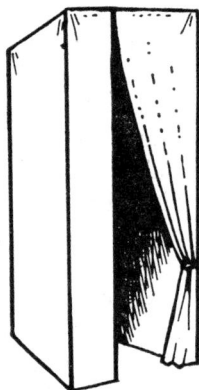

Fig. 53

All in all, modern portable toilets are first-class.

Having purchased your closet, what do you do with it? The answer is the toilet tent. Usually about six feet high and built round a frame, they are manufactured by most leading tent makers and shown in their catalogues. They are not expensive and can be obtained in the same colours as frame tents (see Fig. 53).

The snag once more is space. To carry this form of toilet you require a large car, a luggage or tent trailer, or a caravan. If your car is full and you cannot fit in a portable toilet, you should choose sites with sanitation facilities.

Final Tips on Buying

What have we to look for when buying camping equipment? It must do the job we require it to, it must be easy to erect and it must be safe when erected. You should check all these points as it is important to save labour when pitching camp. No matter how good an article may be when assembled, it should not be purchased if it prolongs your pitching time by any extent. Travelling with the dread of a lengthy stint of pitching before you can ruin your holiday. Also look for double stitching on the canvas or material of your chairs; material tacked to wooden frames tends to pull away. Naturally, you will check the strength of joints and stability.

Chapter 7

Cooking, Heating and Lighting

As there is such a wide variety of apparatus for cooking, heating and lighting purposes, I think it will be best if I discuss each type under the heading of the particular fuel it uses.

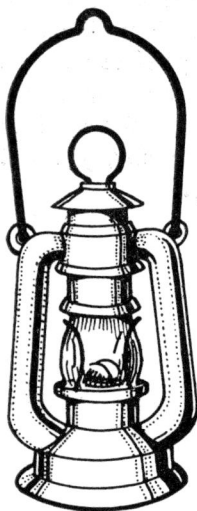

Fig. 54

Paraffin

This is the traditional fuel. The old-fashioned wick lamps give little trouble and cause little smell if kept clean, and simply require a match to light them (see Fig. 54). They need no description from me, but as they give only limited heat they are no longer popular in camp. This, however, does not apply to the pressure version. There are several very good makes on the market, but by far the best-known name is that of Primus. Thus, although it is incorrect, this type of heater, no matter who manufactures it, has become known as a "Primus".

The apparatus works by pumping liquid paraffin from the tank, which is usually the base of the heater, into a coil of tubes which is pre-heated by burning methylated spirit or solid fuel in a small trough situated below or beside the tubes. This vaporises the paraffin, which can easily be lighted at the jet. The heater is so arranged that, once it is burning, it automatically heats the fresh paraffin supply as it is drawn from the tank (see Fig. 55). There are two basic types of stove – the silent type and that which is known as the "roarer". The latter is somewhat noisy, but is better in windy conditions (experienced light-weight campers usually prefer this type).

Maintenance

1. Keep the jet clean and only use the correct pressure.
2. Always light up by using methylated spirit or solid fuel.
3. When dismantling the stove – particularly the folding type which is dismantled regularly – use spanners of the correct

Fig. 55

size. Damage can be caused by using the wrong tools.
4. Check the washers at all points, especially where the apparatus is jointed to the tank and where the vaporiser joins the heater at the methylated spirit trough. Keep a supply of spare washers and change them whenever you have the slightest doubt.
5. Check the seal inside the filler cap. If this is worn the pressure will be lost.
6. Good stoves have a pressure valve; do not mess about with this.

If kept clean and regularly maintained, the paraffin pressure stove will give years of safe and trouble-free ser-

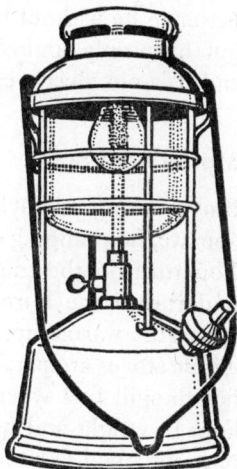

vice. If, on the other hand, the apparatus is allowed to get dirty and the washers are not renewed as necessary, you are liable to get spectacular flare-ups. Even if these are not as frightening as they sound and sometimes look, it is better to be without them. These stoves are cheap to run, but have only limited adjustment. Paraffin can be spilt, and it is not always easy to obtain on the Continent.

Methylated Spirit

Stoves using methylated spirit are cheap and easy to operate, no pumping or pricking of the jet being required. You turn on the fuel, which appears in a small trough underneath the burner, and put a match to it. As the apparatus warms up, the spirit burns in the jet like gas. These stoves are particularly safe, providing you take care not to spill fuel when filling up. They are also efficient, light in weight and use only a little fuel. There is no unpleasant smell. The best-known make is TURM.

Petrol

My comments regarding paraffin apply equally to petrol. Petrol burns with a hot flame, and the apparatus is usually better controlled and adjusted than a paraffin cooker. The stove is safe if used correctly (see Fig. 56). It must, however, be remembered that petrol can be dangerous stuff if mishandled.

Leaded petrol should not be used for cooking or lighting unless there is first-class ventilation which can be guaranteed to remove all fumes. In this case the danger is not great, but as these conditions are rare in a tent it is inadvisable to use it. In addition, it leaves a deposit on

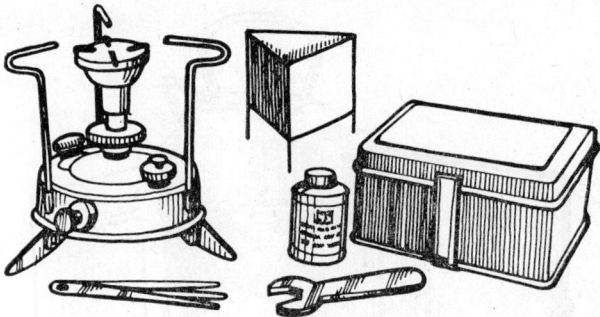

Fig. 56

your apparatus. This means, therefore, that you cannot use the petrol from your car. Unleaded petrol has to be ordered specially, but any garage will obtain it for you.

Gas

This is the most convenient fuel to use in camp, no priming or constant refilling being necessary. The only exception might be the lightweight camper, who may consider himself better off with a paraffin or meths stove. Gas provides first-class adjustment. Its only disadvantages are the cost of gas refills and the need to be certain that you can obtain a refill when required. The former is not serious, as the amount of gas used on a fortnight's camping holiday by a family of four is comparatively small and the cost in excess of that of spirit is very little. As a rule, the family will find a Camping Gaz 907 container sufficient for a week. The gas (not the container) costs about 80p.

Bottled gas provides cheap, clean and easily carried power. In my opinion, the development in recent years of portable gas cooking facilities has been the main reason why camping has become a respectable form of holiday in

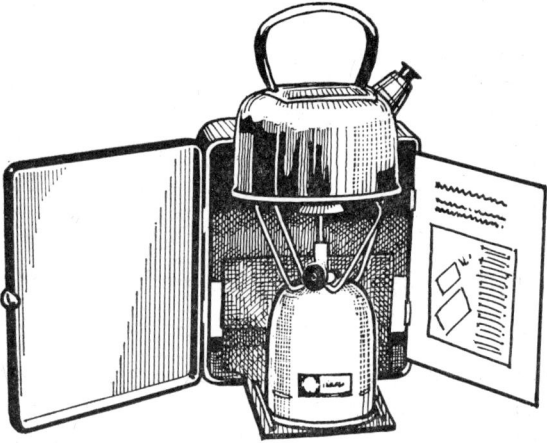

Fig. 57

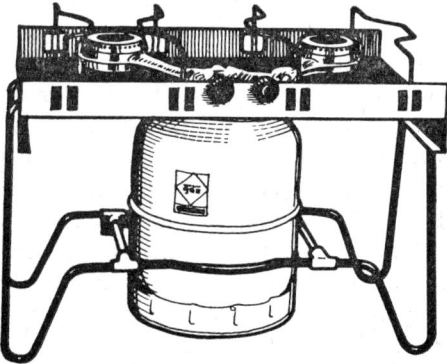

Fig. 58

even the highest circles. I go as far as to put the introduction of gas ahead of the development of frame tents in this respect. The modern gas stove is used like the one we have at home, and it has made all the difference when a man attempts to persuade his wife or girl-friend to go on a camping holiday.

Bottled gas can be used to run cookers (see Figs. 57 and 58), heaters (see Fig. 59), incandescent lights (see Fig. 60),

   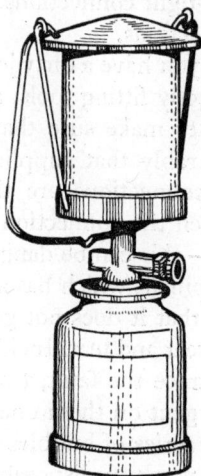

Fig. 59   *Fig. 60*

barbecues, rotisseries and grills. In fact, provided that you are not using the smallest disposal containers, it is possible to use the same container of gas for several types of apparatus as long as you only require one at a time. I have two gas containers – one large and one medium-sized. This permits me to use the former for cooking and to keep the latter as spare or, if we are unfortunate in the weather, to use it for heating. We also carry an incandescent lamp, but only use this if, for some reason, we cannot get the car close to the tent. Our normal form of lighting is electric powered from the car battery (see Fig. 61, page 85).

Gas is just as safe in camp as in the house; the only problems which arise are those resulting from dirt and rough handling. As the gas itself is clean, these difficulties are caused by the camper himself. Most of the fittings are made of brass, and are therefore susceptible to bumps and over-tight connections. Take care not to cross-thread any connections.

If you have a dirty jet or valve, dismantle the part, using correctly fitting tools, and clean it with care (if you use a pricker make sure that you use one of the correct size, preferably that supplied by the maker). Ensure that all the connections are tight, and should you find a leak tighten the connection at once. Never use leaking apparatus – this can be dangerous. Should you have the type of equipment which has a flexible tube as a connection, take care that it does not get damaged, and check it regularly for wear and tear. Incidentally, if you smell a leak and cannot trace the fault, test all the joints by smearing liquid detergent on them one at a time – you will obtain a nice little series of bubbles from the leak.

If you use disposable containers, ensure that the pin which pierces the container is clean and straight, and never take the container off whilst it contains gas. Once removed, keep it away from any naked flame as it could contain a residue of gas.

The Calor Gas Company issue an amusing little booklet called *Playing Safe*. Amongst the points they make are:

1. Ensure that the place in which you use the gas apparatus is well ventilated.

2. Never position a gas container on its side or out of the vertical; always store it upright with the valve at the top.
3. When the gas is not in use, turn it off at the cylinder, as well as the tap on the apparatus.
4. Check that the apparatus taps are off before turning on the tap at the cylinder.
5. If the flame goes out, do not re-light until all the escaped gas (if any) has dispersed.
6. Before changing a cylinder, ensure that the valve is turned off.
7. If there is a pressure regulator, do not interfere with it or attempt to adjust it.

In their Camping Gaz brochure the distributors, the Pneumatic Tent Company Ltd. (P.T.C.), state that they will carry out repairs within two days. I tested this ambitious offer in the busiest time of the year and they fully lived up to their statement – at a very reasonable price, too. It is worth noting that "Camping Gaz" is the only brand of bottled gas available throughout Europe.

High and Low Pressure Gas Stoves
Do not confuse high and low pressure gas stoves with pressure oil and petrol heaters, cookers or lamps. A vapour pressure gas appliance is one which burns at the pressure of the gas in the container. Low pressure appliances operate at a much lower pressure, which is controlled by a reducing valve called a regulator.

Vapour pressure appliances are fitted direct to the container, or are connected by a reinforced hose with a leak-preventing clip at each end. Low pressure apparatus can be connected with a rubber hose which slips onto the feed pipes of the appliance and the container. I also advise a reinforcing clip at each end of the hose on low pressure appliances.

The only real difference in use between the two types as far as the camper is concerned is that the high pressure appliances are less affected by wind and draughts. I do not think that the amount of heat produced in normal conditions is any different.

Gas on a Caravan or Motor Caravan

On a caravan or motor caravan the gas cylinder is usually very large and fixed outside the vehicle, either on the drawbar of the former or, in the case of the latter, on a special fitting. As so much gas is involved, it is definitely better to turn off the gas cylinder when not in use; there is almost certain to be a valve provided on large containers. If the container is inside your motor caravan, care should be taken and the valve always kept off when the gas is not being used.

Gas on the Channel Crossing

The rules regarding gas containers on Channel crossings are very strict, although they do vary from port to port and between shipping lines. The number of cylinders carried is limited and they have to be adequately secured against movement; in many cases cylinders have to be declared in advance. Pierced expendable containers cannot be taken and partly-used containers of the non-expendable type will be tested. These are only a few of the regulations; but in case they appear rather off-putting it should be mentioned that no one I know has ever declared gas cylinders or has ever been questioned regarding them – perhaps they have been lucky.

Electricity

So far, I have not come across any form of electric cooker for campers, although kettles which plug into the car battery are available. Electric lighting, however, is very popular, current being supplied by dry battery or the car battery. Dry batteries tend to run out at critical moments

Fig. 61

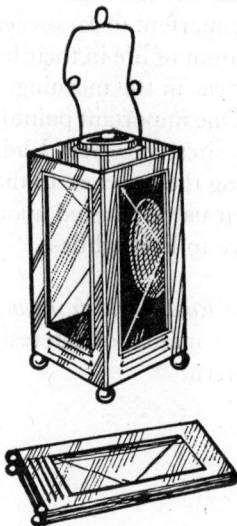

Fig. 62

and at times when shops are closed; in addition, they are large things to carry about if you are using a decent-sized lamp. This leaves lamps connected to the car battery (see Fig. 61). Many types can be connected to either car or dry batteries and this is very convenient.

Electric lights are very good, and come in many shapes

and sizes. I use a car headlamp bulb connected to a live point on my dashboard and so arranged as to be on full beam. This gives first-class light, and the live point avoids having to open the bonnet and getting dirty whilst linking up with the car battery terminals. Commercial electric lights have fittings that hang from the ridge pole or clip onto an upright. The latest thing is the fluorescent tube. This uses less current for the same amount of light, which is important to car owners who might be worried about the amount of life in their battery being insufficient to start up the car in the morning. It is, however, rather expensive.

One important point for electric light enthusiasts – there are sites, very few I admit, where it is not permitted to bring the car close to the tent. Car parks are provided and their use is insisted upon. If you strike such a site you will have to live lightless.

The Really Old-fashioned
As a matter of interest, Fig. 62 shows a folding candle lantern.

Chapter 8

The Trailer Caravan

People take up caravan touring for a variety of reasons. Some are tent campers who have simply become tired of erecting and dismantling their fabric homes or who have possibly had a run of bad luck with their weather. I know what it feels like to camp in a tent on muddy ground in wet weather and to compare my lot with that of the caravanner who has no worry about rain or draught. Others are attracted by the 'vans on display at exhibitions or perhaps are influenced by friends. I am not concerned with the many holiday-makers who hire a 'van at a particular site or with people who use one as a permanent home.

Very well, having opted for a caravan, you have two decisions to make: how big is it to be and where are you going to keep it? Assuming that you have an average-sized car, you will be able to pull ten- or twelve-footers without difficulty.

When buying their first caravan, most people think in terms of a small 'van, such as a ten-footer (see Fig. 63). These are reasonably priced and easy to tow, and many are extremely well fitted out. However, experienced 'van owners with whom I have discussed the matter are all agreed that only a twelve-footer will do for them – especially for a family with one or two children. If you buy a small 'van, you will almost certainly become dissatisfied with it within a year or so and will want a larger one. Fortunately, small 'vans hold their value well and you will be able to part-exchange them without any great financial loss. But it may be a good idea to get the bigger model in the first place – or you could go even larger (see Fig. 64).

Fig. 63

If you do, you will begin to tow quite a weight and charges will be higher should you take your 'van abroad. On the other hand, it is obvious that the larger the 'van, the more room you have inside it. However, since one goes touring to see the countryside, the 'van is used mainly for eating and sleeping. So, providing you can cook, eat and sleep in reasonable comfort, and have room to sit and read if it rains, that is about all the space you require. Don't forget that you will only be using your caravan at weekends and for two or three weeks in the summer so that the room you expect at home is not necessary.

A caravan need not be expensive; you can buy one second-hand in good condition for a very reasonable sum. I would not advise buying a very old one as suspension and towing behaviour have improved out of all recognition in

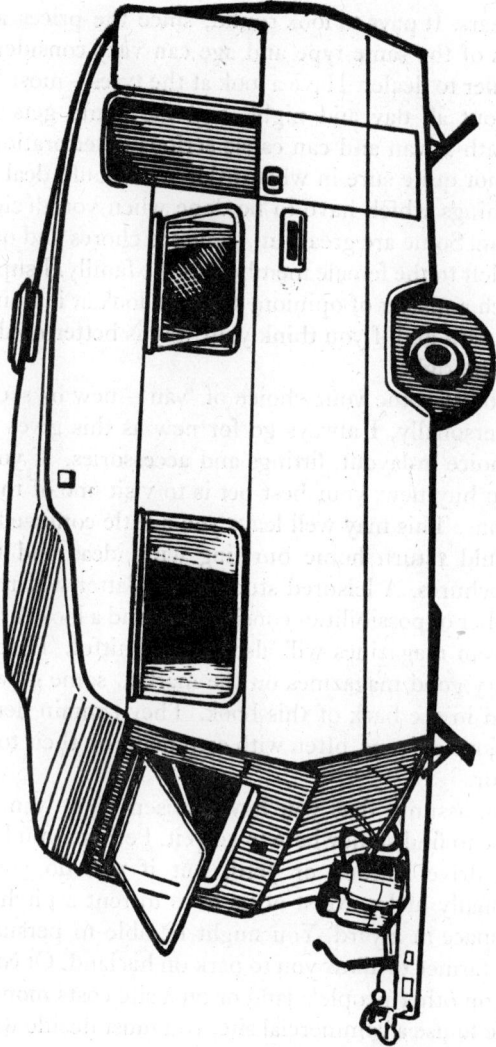

Fig. 64

recent years. It pays to look round, since the prices asked for 'vans of the same type and age can vary considerably from dealer to dealer. Have a look at the tyres – most 'vans are left out all day and night, and the damp gets right underneath a 'van and can cause serious deterioration.

I am not quite sure in what order you should deal with all the things which have to be done when you decide to buy a 'van. Some are great fun, some are chores and others are best left to the female members of the family. I suppose it is much a matter of opinion, so I will look at it from my point of view and if you think your way is better no doubt you will be right.

First must come your choice of 'van – new or second-hand? Personally, I always go for new as this gives a far wider choice in layout, fittings and accessories. If you do decide to buy new, your best bet is to visit one of the big exhibitions. This may well leave you a little confused, but you should return home bursting with ideas and laden with brochures. A leisured study of the latter will reduce the number of possibilities considerably and a look through the caravan magazines will also prove fruitful. There are some very good magazines on the market, some of which are listed in the back of this book. They contain detailed descriptions of 'vans, often with comments on their towing behaviour.

Let us assume that you have chosen your 'van. You now have to find somewhere to keep it. Perhaps you have a suitable drive, garden or yard, but if you do you are exceptionally lucky. Most of us have to rent a pitch on a site or space in a yard. You might be able to persuade a friendly farmer to allow you to park on his land. Of course, parking on other people's land or on a site costs money. If you have to use a commercial site, you must decide whether to choose one near home, irrespective of its scenic position, so that it is convenient for the start of your tours, or whether to find a site on which you will be happy to spend your weekends, which will probably mean having the 'van some distance from home. Your dealer will usually be able and willing to assist you with information about sites, but in any case there are the caravan clubs whose function it is to assist you – naturally they expect you to join them, which is only fair.

The choice of 'van and the decision to buy it is rather like the launching of a ship: the general public tend to consider the work finished when the 'van is delivered, whereas in truth at this stage you have only the basic fabric and the essential fittings. You now have to undertake the fitting out. This is either very enjoyable or infuriating, according to your temperament; it is also to a great extent the work of Mrs. and Miss Caravanner. First, make a careful check on the 'van, ensuring that everything listed as supplied is actually there. Also look for such items as faulty paintwork or ill-fitting doors; these will be put right by the dealer. Make sure that all the metal pins and screws which hold the panelling in place are fully embedded and covered over; if any protrude, they will rust as condensation forms in the 'van and in time cause unsightly stains on the panels. Condensation is a nuisance and in extreme cases can cause damage. It will pay you to go round the 'van and make a note of any weak points in insulation – the floor and wheel arches will often reveal faults. Material of the type used for ceiling tiles provides first-class insulation, but make sure you use the non-inflammable type. The floor is a major job and you may well be advised to seek expert advice on this.

When fitting out it does not matter where you start, but

as you have to sleep and eat in the 'van let us consider the beds first and then the cooking facilities.

The Beds

Preparing for bed is a major operation and it is essential, or at least very helpful, to develop a system. Many caravanners keep the bedding for each particular bunk in the space beneath it. This entails disturbing only the particular bunk which you wish to prepare at the time. Other people prefer to store all the bedding in one bunk so that the spare space beneath the others is available for clothing and so on. You have the choice of blankets or sleeping bags, but I personally prefer the latter as they save bed making and tucking in.

The storage of clothing is closely linked with sleeping; larger items are no real problem, but it is a nuisance to have to search frantically for socks and other small things. It is easy to make a hold-all, which hangs on the inside of the wardrobe door, with pockets for such small things and possibly toilet items as well.

The Kitchen

Reduce the number of utensils to a minimum and choose the type which will fit into the drawers provided for storage. Also select a bowl which fits the sink for washing up and washing; this saves a great deal of water – it is amazing how much water can be used in a day if you use the sink itself all the time. You require a bucket to collect water from your sink outlet, since this simply empties out on to the ground below the 'van, and fresh water containers. You need two of the latter so that one is always full, but attempt to obtain the type which will fit somewhere inside your 'van.

Should the manufacturer have failed to provide a permanent place for your gas container, it will pay you to find one yourself. If you fit it inside, drill a few holes in the floor round it; gas is heavier than air and these holes will allow it to escape in the event of a leak. The obvious, and probably the best, place for the gas cylinder is on the drawbar of the van. You can obtain special holders for fitting your cylinders in this position from either the caravan supplier or the gas supplier.

The manufacturer should provide suitable places for the storage of crockery. There will probably be spaces for cups, saucers and plates, so choose crockery which fits. Also ensure that the cupboard doors close properly and that they will stay closed when the 'van is on the road. Cupboard doors are a weakness in many 'vans and it is annoying to find nothing more than broken pieces of crockery when you reach your chosen site.

A collection of screw-top jars and plastic bags is ideal for groceries and greengroceries. Storing glass jars and tumblers is a problem. Get hold of some thick sponge rubber or polystyrene and cut holes in it to fit your jars and glasses; stick thin sponge rubber under the holes and you have a first-class holder. It pays to keep jars and bottles near to or on the floor as they are heavy when filled. Polythene is tremendously useful to caravanners. Bread, cakes, salt, pepper, tea, sugar, etc., can all be kept in polythene packs. They are light, strong, airtight and completely waterproof. You can even carry peeled potatoes and water in such containers. Use plastic buckets for waste, keeping one colour for dry waste and another for wet waste materials. This is necessary as sites often provide separate collection points for wet and dry waste matter.

The Toilet

How essential a personal toilet is to the caravanner is a matter of opinion; possibly it depends on the type of touring undertaken. If you are sticking to established, well-equipped sites you will not require your own facilities. On the other hand, all those who regard themselves as "genuine touring caravanners" insist on carrying their own toilet arrangements, either built into the 'van or in the form of the separate toilet tent, which I have already described briefly in Chapter 6, page 74. The majority have the built-in "little room". The popular brands of 'van are supplied with this compartment empty, leaving you to furnish it. As a rule, you have the choice of a small 'van without a toilet compartment or a larger vehicle complete in this respect. If you have a small car, the best choice may well be a small 'van and a separate toilet tent.

My comments on furnishing the 'van's toilet apply equally to a toilet tent. Portable toilets are essentially chemical, by far the most common type being basically a pack containing water mixed with a fluid. This "preserves" the contents inoffensively until you can dispose of them. Some sites, but by no means all, have disposal points. You can buy cheap toilets made of treated metal, but in my opinion, however well these are treated, rust will appear in time, so you may consider it better to pay more for an all-plastic model. Secure sealing of the toilet is vital – you must have it tightly closed when the van is on tow. You also require a model which has a lid to close the bucket when it is being taken to the emptying point. Before you finally buy, measure up and ensure that it will fit the compartment when in use. As a rule, the more luxurious your toilet, the more room it requires. A detail often forgotten is a receptacle for toilet paper. A flat pack is usually more convenient than a roll.

One final comment on this subject: I have mentioned the emptying point – very often there will not be one if you are caravanning on your own. In this case you will require a tool to dig a pit. There are many collapsible types of spades and entrenching tools on sale which are effective and take up very little space.

The Awning

Most caravanners use an awning, which is usually specially built to fit each particular 'van (see Fig. 65). It can be

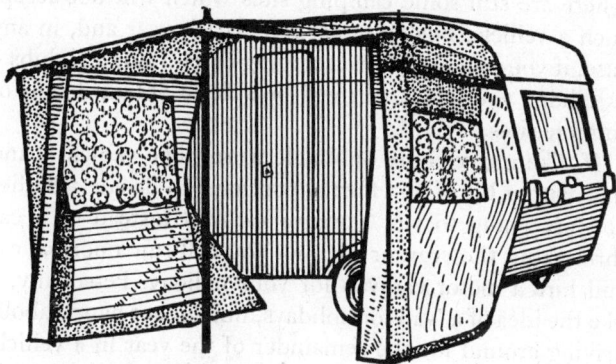

Fig. 65

closed down and used to sleep people who cannot be accommodated in the 'van – just like a tent. Alternatively, it can be used open as a sun awning.

Chapter 9

The Motor Caravan

The motor caravan is one of the four great innovations of modern camping, the others being the frame tent, the trailer tent and cooking by gas. It is a wonderful way of camping. You have the comforts of the best-equipped trailer caravan without any of the problems of towing. There are still some camping sites which will not accept such a vehicle, but these get fewer each year and, in any case, if you join one of the camping or caravanning clubs – as I hope you will – you will be able to obtain details of suitable sites.

If, like me, you are only able to run one vehicle – and that with a bit of an effort – you have to decide whether you are going to run a motor caravan instead of a car throughout the year, or whether you will run a normal car and hire a motor caravan for your holiday. Personally, I like the idea of a 'van for holidays, but am not happy about driving around for the remainder of the year in a vehicle which looks something like an ice-cream van. At best, it looks like a commercial vehicle and, of course, drives like one. I always think that a motor caravan rally looks from a distance like an ice-cream sellers' convention. This is rather unfair, however, because the shape is the result of necessity. Designers have achieved a miracle of design inside the vehicle in order to provide complete comfort in a very small space.

If you decide to buy a motor caravan, what choices are

available? Here are a few points to bear in mind. Do not rush around to the nearest agent and buy the first 'van which takes your fancy. You may buy just the vehicle which suits you, but, with about a hundred different models to choose from, you are far more likely to finish with one which does not match up to your requirements. I do not think there are any really bad designs on the market, it is simply a matter of finding one which fits in with your own ideas of perfection. The different models vary considerably in layout, driving performance and, of course, price.

Most motor caravans are based on medium-sized commercial vans. The type usually selected for conversions is the 15-cwt model with a 1700-cc engine or thereabouts. The result is a bed-sitter with an engine stuck on the front to move it from place to place, and you have to balance your requirements as a camper with those as a motorist. Nevertheless, the range is very wide indeed, from the 8-cwt Ford Escort to the 2½-ton Mercedes.

All motor caravans seat from four to six persons in varying degrees of comfort. In order to be taxed and insured as a private vehicle, the 'van must not have more than eight seats plus the driver or weigh more than 8 tons. To obtain exemption from Purchase Tax there must be one 6-ft bed, storage for 6 gallons of water, a wardrobe and cooking facilities. This puts some limitation on the designer, but still leaves room for much variation. The conversion experts use a variety of chassis, including Bedford, Ford, B.L.M.C., Land Rover, Commer and Volkswagen. Naturally, the smaller the chassis, the less room there is in the caravan. You must expect to spend from £1000, for which you have a reasonable choice of good-quality products, to an almost unlimited amount for really luxury vehicles.

Obviously, the number of people intending to use the 'van decides to a great extent the layout of the interior for you. If it is a family affair, you may well think that the type of roof is the first decision to be made. There are two basic types of 'van: those which retain the body of a standard van and those with a completely new coachwork body specially built for the purpose. All types of 'van fall into one of these two groups.

Most common is the conversion of a standard commercial van. These usually, but not always, have an "elevating" roof fitted. This is a rising section built into the fixed roof of the normal van. Often this accommodates one or two stretcher beds. Naturally, the bedding and so on used in the rising section has to be stored elsewhere when

Fig. 66

the roof is lowered (see Figs. 66 and 67). If, therefore, you choose this type of 'van, your first decision is whether or not you want a rising roof. As, even when lowered, this slightly raises the height of the 'van, it may result in its not fitting your garage. However, I think you must be able to

Fig. 67

stand upright in your 'van and therefore consider a rising roof to be essential.

Amongst the motor caravans which are based on standard vehicles are the recently introduced "car-sized" type. If you have to run your 'van as a private car for the remainder of the year, this may be the answer to your problem. Amongst these are the Dormobile Roma, based on the Bedford, and the Escort van conversion. The coach-built motor caravans have specially built bodies which give comfortable standing room without the need for a rising roof and more inside space than is found in the standard van body. As a rule, a coach-built 'van is more luxurious than the van-bodied conversion. At most, this can accommodate two people and a child, but if your family consists of no more than this, or if you are willing to use a tent as well, it may be your answer, providing as it does caravan accommodation in a vehicle which looks very much like the ordinary shooting-brake type of car. The

Dormobile Roma, for example, stands only $5\frac{1}{2}$ ft high and is $12\frac{1}{2}$ ft long, but can sleep, as I have said, two adults on a 6-ft double bed and a child; it even includes a fold-away cooker and sink unit. You can get some idea of its size if you remember that, whilst the average motor cara-van is built on a 15-cwt chassis, the Roma has a 8-cwt Bed-ford as a basis. Although it does not have the performance of a private car, it is quite convenient for town driving and will fit in the normal-sized family garage (see Fig. 68).

Fig. 68

Another similar mini motor caravan is based on the Ford Escort (see Fig. 69). Naturally, the fittings – which include a grill, wardrobe, cupboards and water carriers – are small and the space very limited, but the designers have wasted hardly an inch of their restricted living area.

Beds in motor caravans are very important. How many is easy to decide, but how they make up varies consider-

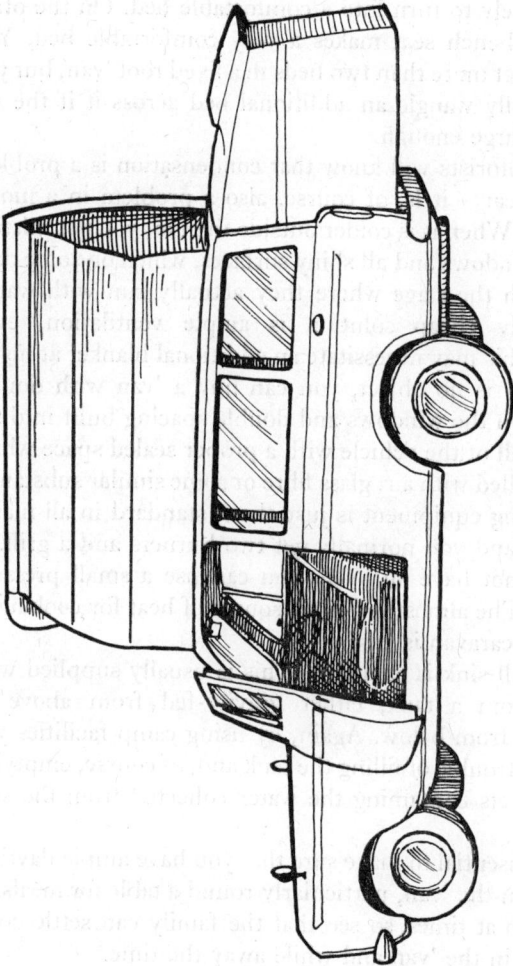

Fig. 69

ably. If you insist on first-class driving seats in front, they are unlikely to turn into a comfortable bed. On the other hand, a bench seat makes a very comfortable bed. You seldom get more than two beds in a fixed roof 'van, but you can usually wangle an additional bed across it if the vehicle is large enough.

All motorists will know that condensation is a problem in their car – it is, of course, also a problem in a motor caravan. When it is colder outside than in, you get misting up on windows and all shiny surfaces, which on some days can reach the stage where they actually run with water. The only cheap solution is ample ventilation, even though this may necessitate an additional blanket at night. If money is no object, you can buy a 'van with double glazing on the windows and double spacing built into the body shell of the vehicle with a proper sealed space which will be filled with air, glass fibre or some similar substance.

Cooking equipment is just about standard in all makes of 'van, and you normally get two burners and a grill. If you do not have an oven, you can use a small pressure cooker. The almost universal source of heat for cooking in a motor caravan is gas.

A small sink is standard. This is usually supplied with water from a tank, either gravity-fed from above or pumped from below. Again, by using camp facilities you save the trouble of filling the tank and, of course, emptying the buckets containing the water collected from the sink outlet.

It is essential to make sure that you have ample daytime seating in the 'van, particularly round a table for meals. It does rain at times, so see that the family can settle comfortably in the 'van and while away the time.

Some models are equipped with a built-in chemical

toilet, but it saves considerable trouble if the site toilets are used.

Extra equipment is always a problem. Whatever you do, don't clutter up your 'van with items that it is not really worth taking. Before buying any new equipment you should plan where it is going to go. Provided you do not have a rising roof, there is usually a roof rack which will fit your 'van, and even some elevated roof types will take a rack.

I am sure that once you have had a little experience of motor caravanning you will want an awning. This is virtually a frame tent which is attached to the 'van. It can be designed specially for your particular model, being erected so that there is direct entrance to the awning from the exit of the 'van. If you buy your awning with sides and a front, you have a complete tent which can sleep members of the family or friends. Alternatively, you can simply use it as a sunshade under which you can sit and eat in fine weather. The awning is complete in itself in that it can be left up whilst you are away in the 'van.

How Does a Motor Caravan Compare with a Car?

The price is much the same. You expect to pay more for the fittings and the special design included in a motor caravan, but this is compensated for by its being free of Purchase Tax. If you are prepared to drive such a vehicle for the remainder of the year, you have quite a few advantages over the car owner. You have a car and a travelling home. Children can move about and play games at the table en route. (I must say here that I am a strong believer in seat belts, so I do not like children or adults moving about whilst the vehicle is moving. I think they should be securely belted into their seats, but these can still be at the table.) There is plenty of leg room for adults and space for baggage, every piece being, of course, in its proper place and readily available. The driving position is first-class. You are high up and usually well forward so that you have a far better field of vision than the car driver. As the vehicles are designed for commercial drivers, you should find the driving seat very comfortable once you have become used to the more upright position.

The motor caravan, being based on a commercial vehicle, is built for rough use and is expected to live outside. It is therefore tough and long-lasting. As a result, you can expect trouble-free motoring for a long time and should be able to cover rough ground without difficulty. Although wider and higher, few motor caravans are longer than a car. This is a great advantage because it enables you to take your 'van abroad by air or sea at no extra cost to a car.

Tax and insurance cost no more, and there is no special speed limit – at least that is the view of the Motor Caravanners Club. When you insure, it is worth including an additional clause to cover the use of gas. As a rule, a motor caravan is treated as a private car by car park and traffic authorities.

What, then, is there against the motor caravan as a vehicle? Well, it is a biggish commercial vehicle and handles as such. Being high and wide, it is naturally more susceptible to wind than a car. It is not as fast and has less acceleration. The engine does have a fairly high noise level, which can be tiring to the driver, but this can be overcome to a great extent by putting sleeping bags or blankets on the engine cover – providing, of course, that it is inside the driving cab of the vehicle.

Your main decision is whether you can face driving a

motor caravan for business and all the time when you are
not camping. You will be left at traffic lights, and a motor
caravan will not be as handy as a car when it comes to
parking. You will have to convince your wife that this is a
suitable mode of transport for shopping or visiting friends,
which is something that I shall never be able to do. If,
however, you have all these points well in hand, it is worth
considering buying a motor caravan when the time next
comes for a new car.

Camping in Car Parks and on Verges

I am not an expert on the law, but have looked up a few
points which will be of interest to motor caravanners. An
acquaintance of mine merely drives into the town car park
and stays overnight. The legal position appears to be that,
if you pay to park on such land, you make a contract which
is based on the conditions which are usually displayed.
These are easily enforced during the day when an attend-
ant is present, but what if you arrive late and leave early?
The odds are that you would get away with it, but legally
the owners could bring an action and sue for damages for
trespass.

Some motor caravanners have got into the habit of
parking at night on the grass verges near towns or beauty
spots; others use lay-bys for spending the night. At present, this does not appear to be an offence, although many
councils are quite rightly attempting to take action to prevent this objectionable habit. Even if it is not illegal, it is
certainly bad manners to park on anyone's land without
permission. This includes roadside verges since they are
part of the road. Lay-bys are for resting for short periods.
Move on if you are requested to do so, leaving no trace

of your occupation, as you have no rights in the matter unless you are on private land with the owner's permission.

Building Your Own 'Van

Information regarding a do-it-yourself motor caravan can be obtained from the motor caravan clubs and magazines, so I do not propose to go into this in any great detail. The idea of a do-it-yourself effort is to be able to convert a van of your own choice into a caravan which meets your personal needs. All the accessories, including a lifting roof, can be purchased, the success of the job depending on the time available and your skill.

Remember that the space available in the 'van is limited, so anything that you decide to put in it is usually included at the expense of something else. A list of items desired has to be built up and then put into order of priority. If you have a door at the side of the vehicle, you will have to design a layout quite different from that required for a rear-door model. Lay out your design on paper, working to scale. Draw the outline of the interior and cut sections of cardboard to represent the base of each item, such as bed, table, cooker, etc., to exact scale. In this way you will see how much space is available.

Do not start planning until you have looked over all the 'vans you can find. Many makes are now on display at the various exhibitions and you will be able to build up a considerable library of caravan plans, from which you should succeed in planning your own ideal vehicle.

Before you commence work, you must write to your local Customs and Excise Office. They will supply a leaflet which will detail the requirements for a motor caravan. This will avoid finding yourself liable for Purchase Tax.

Part Three

Care of Equipment

Chapter 10

Maintaining Your Tent and Trailer Tent

When you obtain your new tent or trailer tent from your dealer, it should be in perfect condition and capable of providing many years of hard wear – and so it will if treated with care. In the few cases of which I have heard where a new tent has proved faulty, the faults have been corrected or the tent exchanged with no trouble and little delay. Exactly how long your tent lasts is, therefore, entirely up to you.

The first thing to remember is that any fabric put away dirty and damp will come to harm. You would not dream of putting clothing away in that state, so why pack up an expensive tent that has not been cleaned and dried out properly? Before dismantling your tent, remove dust and dirt from the sewn-in groundsheet, brush off any leaves, pieces of twig (these cut), insects or grit on the outside of the fabric, and sponge off bird droppings and mud (only clean water should be used as soap or detergent will remove the proofing). Wipe off any mud on the plastic skirting of the tent and the underside of the groundsheet. The latter is almost certain to be wet, since it draws up moisture from the ground, and must be allowed to dry out before it is finally packed away. The frame sections should also be cleaned if they are muddy. Always try to pack a dry tent; if by waiting an hour or so before breaking camp on the last day you can allow the dew or morning damp on the fabric to dry out, do so. If you are not completely certain that the tent is dry, spread it out at home or put it up again in the garden to air.

If you have put up your tent correctly – i.e. in the way the manufacturer intended it to be erected – ensuring that the frame touches only the reinforced parts of the fabric and that no section is too tight or too loose, and packed it away carefully after use, you are well on the way to avoiding any necessity for repair. But what specifically can cause the condition of your tent to deteriorate?

The following can damage a tent:

1. Wind.
2. Rain.
3. Sunlight.
4. Mildew.
5. Dust.
6. The ground on which you pitch.
7. Cooking (inside the tent).
8. Hail or snow (if you go in for winter camping).
9. Carelessness.

Let us take each of the above in turn and see exactly how they can affect the life of a tent.

1 *Wind*. Wind causes movement in the tent so that the frame flexes and gives, and in turn tightens and loosens the fabric, stretching it and allowing it to bag with each gust. Each movement strains the material and reduces its strength. As the wind moves the fabric, it rubs against the frame and can catch on any sharp article within reach. However, it is not only the pressure of the wind that causes damage – it also drives rain, grit and dust into the fabric.

2 *Rain*. Rain blown in a gale can exert terrific pressure on

the material; it also carries chemicals which are deposited on the fabric and left as the tent dries. You have only to think how dirty a clean car can get after rain to envisage how your tent could be damaged. If your tent is well proofed, however, there will be little danger from this source. But, should the canvas not be quite taut, puddles of rain will form on the roof of the tent and the awning, and the weight of water will stretch the fabric. Do not allow puddles to form, therefore, or at least disperse them as soon as possible.

3 *Sunlight*. As everybody knows, sunlight causes dyes to fade; rain speeds up the process. You can only prevent fading by avoiding the sun, and no one, I imagine, will wish to do that. A yellow or green tent will keep its original colour longer than one which is orange or blue. But since the faded tent is the mark of the experienced camper, you may consider it desirable for the prestige it gives you as an old hand.

4 *Mildew*. In practice, there is only danger from this source when a tent is packed away damp. But should mildew form it can spell the beginning of the end of your expensive tent. Mildew is caused by spores, and the ideal conditions for rapid growth include water, warmth and darkness. The more of these conditions you can remove when storing your tent, the less likelihood there is of mildew spreading.

5 *Dust*. This is often overlooked when the useful life of a tent is considered. Dust is a very serious menace to the fabric in hot, dry climates and in a wind can be blown across the face of the fabric with the effect of sandpaper. Dust should be removed before a tent is packed away.

6 *The ground on which you pitch.* This is important; rough ground can cause a tent to be badly pitched, which will mean that the fabric is unevenly distributed and will collect puddles if it rains, placing an unnecessary strain on the material. Uneven ground also puts undue strain on the zips and can even twist the frame. Take care not to pitch on stones or sticks as these can tear the sewn-in groundsheet.

7 *Cooking inside the tent or close to the fabric outside the tent.* Unless you are very careful and lucky, you cannot cook inside the tent or outside close to the tent wall without splashing the fabric with fat or other foods. Fat not only makes ugly stains on the material but also greatly increases the danger of mildew. To remove fat or food stains you should wash the fabric in clean water. Some tents are supplied with kitchen compartments or have them available as an optional extra. A few of these provide protection for the tent material by covering the inside of the tent wall with plastic. If your tent has no such protection, you can fix a sheet of transparent plastic to the fabric by gluing strips of velcro to the plastic and stitching the other part of the velcro to the tent material (your stitching should be done along a seam).

8 *Hail and snow.* I suppose very few of my readers will expect to get caught in hail or snow storms during their camping holidays. However, many families and canoeists camp throughout the year, and others may well run into unseasonable weather. Naturally, it is always better to pitch your tent in a sheltered spot – especially when the weather is doubtful – but it is just about impossible to protect the tent completely. Hail is a menace because it can be belted like bullets against the tent and the camper cannot do much to stop this. If, however, hail and ice are

swept from the fabric as soon as possible, this will prevent the weight pulling the material out of shape.

Snow presents much the same problem. Whilst it will not damage the tent by beating against it, the weight of snow can do considerable damage – even bending the frame in extreme cases. Snow must be removed from the tent as it falls; do not wait until the end of the snowstorm.

9 *Carelessness.* I suppose more damage is done to tents by sheer carelessness than by lack of knowledge. Sharp objects left under the groundsheet or the mud flaps will cut the material, and trees overlapping the tent drop dusty rain or sticky matter on the roof fabric – in fact, branches which seem a fair way away in calm weather can be driven through the fabric as soon as the wind becomes fairly strong. Camp furniture left against the tent will rub in even mildly windy conditions, causing extra wear and strain. Children can cause damage with balls, aeroplanes, and bows and arrows; if children other than your own play too near your tent, ask them politely to move a little farther away.

Inspecting Your Tent for Damage

Nothing is more annoying than to arrive at your chosen and eagerly anticipated site only to find that you are short of an essential piece of equipment, or that a vital part of your tent is damaged. If this happens to you, it is entirely your own fault. You should have made a note of any damage to your tent when cleaning and dismantling it after each trip, and if your tent is new you should have put it up as soon as possible after purchase – certainly allowing sufficient time to take up the question of faults with your suppliers or the manufacturer.

These are the points you should check as you take down your tent, especially when breaking camp for the last time of the season:

1. That you have sufficient pegs and that none of them is broken or badly bent.

2. That the rubber loops are sound and not perished.

3. That the guys are sound and the slides, if they are wooden, are not cracked or broken. Should the guys be made of rubber or elastic, see that they have not perished or been cut by metal pegs.

4. That the loops which connect the guys to the tent itself are sound and the stitching is unbroken.

5. Should any part of the tent be eyeleted, either by metal rings or stitching, check that the eyelets are in good order. Should the stitching break or a metal eyelet come out, the stitching can be torn very easily. These eyelets are usually found where an upright pole is designed to hold the corner of the main or window awning, or where a section of the frame which holds the awning links with the main frame.

6. That the zip fasteners are in good order. Ensure that they all close fully and run freely, and that they are still stitched to the fabric all the way along. Wax them from time to time (the easiest and cleanest way is to rub them with an ordinary wax candle). This applies even when your zips are made of plastic. Cut off loose threads of cotton to ensure that the zip cannot jam. Zips are vitally important as they provide you with warmth and privacy. In any case, a flapping doorway can cause damage to the tent in a wind.

7. That the frame of the tent is in good order. See that all the springs which link the frame sections are present and unbroken. As far as the strength of the frame is concerned, these springs play a negligible part, if any part at all, but they do make it simpler to erect the tent. Replacement springs are cheap, and so is the simple tool which enables you to position new springs without difficulty. Once you are familiar with the tent, you may think the lack of a few springs immaterial; this is a matter of opinion. See that none of the frame tubes is bent. A slight curve will make very little difference, but too much curve can seriously weaken the frame's resistance to wind. The snag is that frame sections tend to bend where they join another section, and this makes joining, and in particular disconnecting, the sections difficult. They can be separated by two people, who each take a section and twist in opposite directions as they pull. If this does not work, place the locked joint on a solid base, such as a tree stump or large stone, and tap lightly with a mallet, twisting the sections in opposite directions as you do so.

A commonly overlooked but simple item is checking that the joints of the frame are free from dirt and rust. What happens is that, as the tent is erected or dismantled, the open joints – especially those which dig into the ground when the frame is on its knees – get filled with earth and grass, which hardens and sticks to the metal. The result is that the sections become difficult or even almost impossible to separate.

You may find that the wooden poles supplied with the smaller ridge tents give trouble – either the sections jam together when you come to dismantle the tent, or they are so loose that they tend to become insecure. In the first case, after making sure that the wood is dry, lightly rub down that section of the pole which fits into the metal joint with sandpaper and then apply a coat of varnish. This will prevent water from getting into the wood again and causing it to swell. Should the joint be too loose, you can tighten it by giving the metal joint a few dents with a centre punch. Do this with the wood inside the metal joint, otherwise you will ruin the shape.

8. That the bags which contain your tent poles, etc. are in good repair. If the tent bag is torn, you may find the tent fabric itself catching on some projection. A tear in the peg bag could cause you to lose pegs or, if you wrap the peg bag in your tent, a protruding peg might damage the tent fabric. Finally, whilst it does not much matter if you lose a peg or two through a hole in the bag, it can be a catastrophe to arrive at the site to find that you have lost an important section of the tent frame in this way. My advice is, discard the flimsy bags which are provided with most tents and replace them with army kit-bags (these can be obtained very cheaply at surplus stores).

I seem to have made the inspection rather a major operation – it is really nothing like that at all. You merely look at each guy, loop or eyelet as you pull out the pegs, check the zips as you close them and the frame sections as they are dismantled, and run your finger round the inside of each tube to remove mud and grass as you pack up. It is as easy as that and well worth while. Proper checks and early repairs when necessary will result in the ownership of a tent which will last for years and will have a good part-exchange value. Make any repairs, or have them made, at the time the damage occurs if possible. Most suppliers can arrange your repairs or will do them themselves (the best time is at the end of the season; if you wait until the spring or early summer you will find that everyone else has suddenly remembered jobs that require doing and there may be some delay).

Re-proofing

After a few years, depending on the quality of the fabric and the care which you have taken of it, the outer tent will require re-proofing. This is an easy but essential task. Should rain drip or run through a certain spot in the tent, there is probably a fault or tear in the material, and this should be traced and repaired. Modern lightweight fabrics can be handled easily in a domestic sewing machine. Small holes can be machined and larger ones patched, and seams can be sewn. This, however, is no indication that the tent requires re-proofing. Some experts advise that tents should be re-proofed every two years, but unless you camp almost every weekend I think this is a little too often. How frequently a tent requires re-proofing is very much a matter of quality – that means, in effect, how much you paid. The more expensive fabrics are made of closely woven material, and it is this close weave that keeps the water out. The cheaper material may look as durable and as waterproof as a more expensive one, but this is usually because it is filled up with a proofing agent. The sign that your tent needs re-proofing is when rain comes through in a light spray.

Having made up your mind to re-proof, the first step is to decide which type or brand of re-proofing agent to use. In the old days, there was a tendency for the proofings to dry and fall out. Modern agents are very satisfactory and allow the material to breathe. You have a choice of a wax-based mixture or a silicone solution. The wax may slightly discolour the fabric, but the silicone solution will dry out leaving no trace whatsoever. I am told that the wax also adds to the weight of the fabric, but I don't think any slight increase is worth considering. There is a wide range of brands on the market, many of which claim certain advantageous properties. If you are puzzled, I suggest that you ask your supplier for advice. Special proofing agents are available for rubberised groundsheets, very light tents and clothing. Although directions are usually supplied with packets of proofer, I will run through the procedure, paying attention to points which you may find cause some puzzlement. The job itself is messy and lengthy rather than difficult.

The first step is to make sure that your fabric is clean. You must therefore remove all splashes of mud, grease, mildew and bird droppings. Grease spots can be removed with dry cleaning fluid and the fabric may be washed in warm soapy water (all traces of the soap must, of course, be rinsed off). I strongly advise against using detergents as these only serve to allow water through the fabric. Mildew can be killed with a solution of five tablespoons of sodium hypochlorite to two pints of water. The chemical can be obtained from a chemist and it is washed off with ammonia water. If these chemicals remove the colour from your fabric, use a coloured re-proofer to replace it.

I suppose the job can be carried out indoors, but I would not like to tackle it in this way myself. It is best to undertake the work in the open air with the tent erected, but you must so arrange your timing as to avoid running into unsuitable weather, such as rain, dew or frost. The fabric will take up to twenty-four hours to dry out, and the time and money spent on the work can be wasted if you strike wet weather during the drying period.

Before starting the job, read the directions supplied with the re-proofer carefully. Some have to be diluted with water, but others are used straight out of the container. The proofer can be brushed on with a wide paint brush, and it is best to work to a system dealing with one panel at a time. When each panel has been brushed over with the proofer, rub it over with a clean cloth. This evens out the distribution and is important, when using a coloured proofer, if an uneven result is to be avoided. Should you apply too much of a colourless proofer, you may get a bloom on the fabric, but this can be removed with a cloth moistened with turps substitute.

A very easy method of re-proofing is to use an aerosol spray. You must apply the liquid evenly and avoid a windy day. However, these sprays are expensive and, since you would use up several cans if you attempted to re-proof large patches of the fabric by this method, I would only recommend them for dealing with small patches.

Storing Your Tent

Storing a tent for the winter is easy – put it in a dry place away from moths. I put ours in a kit-bag and, as I use separate bags for the inner and main tent, it is not packed too tightly. I then place the kit-bags in my zip-up roof rack cover, which is damp-proof and moth-proof, and leave the whole lot in our loft. As yet, I have not had any trouble.

Chapter 11

Maintaining Your Caravan and Motor Caravan

Servicing Your Caravan

The life span of a caravan depends entirely on the way it is
looked after by the owner. As most 'vans spend by far the
larger part of the year out of the sight and immediate reach
of their owners, they tend to get neglected and at best receive very scanty servicing. This not only shortens their
life but can also be dangerous. You may therefore consider
it advisable to have your 'van serviced professionally before you go on holiday. I have no experience of this, but if
it is done well it justifies the cost. It is ridiculous to chance
your tour – especially if you are going abroad – being
spoilt by lack of preparation.

I propose to take the major items of servicing one at a
time, but I do not intend to imply that this is the order of
importance – all are equally important.

1 *The hitch and coupling*
These not only maintain contact between your car and
'van, but also apply the brakes and carry the electric connections. The fittings on the car require cleaning. Check
the electric socket and grease the ball, and tighten all the
nuts which hold the towing bracket to the car.

Clean and grease the drawbar on the 'van, and all the

moving parts and pivot points, such as that on the hand-brake. Check the overrun mechanism as far as you can. You cannot actually test it manually, the effort required is too great. If this is too easy to push back you should re-place the damper. Find the grease nipples and use a grease gun on them.

2 Jockey wheel
Check all the moving parts. The clamp screw may well have rusted during the winter, and thus will require de-rusting and cleaning. See that the jockey wheel shaft slides freely.

3 Corner jacks
You must ensure that these work freely. Check that the screws are free of dried mud and grass, and apply thick grease.

4 Under chassis maintenance
Check the tightness of the suspension "U" bolts, and en-sure that the shackles are free of mud and rust. Examine the brake spring leads for breakages. Apply grease to all the nipples.

5 Brakes and wheel bearings
I am not going to explain how brakes should be adjusted because there are several systems and these can differ in detail. Your handbook will explain the procedure as far as your 'van is concerned. You should remove the wheel and inspect the brake linings. If they do not need to be re-placed, dust out and put a tiny spot of grease on the oper-ating mechanism (do not get any grease on the linings as

this will make them ineffective). Check the wheel bearings and grease them if necessary. Now replace the wheel. Finally, tighten up the brakes and then slacken off just sufficiently to allow the wheel to spin. Take the 'van for a run and, having made sure that the road is clear, try an emergency stop. The outfit should pull up in a straight line. Next go steadily for a few miles, using the brakes as little as possible; then roll to a stop and check the 'van brakes for overheating by putting your hand on the drum. If it is cold, you know that you have not over-adjusted the brakes.

It is worth finding out how your 'van's brakes work. The most popular is the "overrun" type. This operates through the drawbar by means of a plunger or piston. As you slow or stop your car, the 'van closes up behind, exerting pressure on the towing apparatus. This forces the plunger down, which operates the brakes. The plunger or piston is normally exposed to the weather and should be kept well greased, and if possible fitted with a cover (these are available from dealers). To reverse it is essential that you prevent the plunger from operating, otherwise you will unintentionally apply the 'van's brakes. To avoid this happening you are provided with a "reverse-stop" lever or, in the case of luggage trailers, with a piece of metal shaped like a "U" which fits onto the piston and prevents it from being compressed. Do not forget to remove this "U" before driving forward again or you will be without any brakes on the 'van.

6 *Roof and bodywork*
Check all joints between panels and fill all gaps with flexible compound. Touch up all breaks in the paintwork, especially in the front which collects mud and stones

thrown up by the car. Check all your hinges and catches on windows, cupboards and ventilators.

7 *Tyres*

Tyres can be a real cause of trouble on tour and few 'vans are supplied complete with a spare. It is worth remembering that a loaded 'van can weigh almost as much as a car and that, whereas a car has four wheels to take the weight, a caravan has only two. The first steps to be taken to preserve your tyres are to keep them correctly inflated and avoid scuffing against or riding over the kerb. Take potholes which you cannot avoid very slowly. During the winter, the 'van should be jacked up to take the weight off the tyres, which should be kept inflated to the correct pressure. Move them around occasionally so that the weight does not bear on the same part all the time (they should really be moved at least once each month).

Although it may help to shield the tyres from direct sunlight, it is not the sun which causes the damage but the air – especially sea air. Whilst a good tyre paint helps for a time, it is not enough. You can cover the tyre in tar-impregnated paper, but an easier method is to obtain an old tyre or an inner tube of larger size. If you use an inner tube, slit the tube all the way round on the inside and then slip it over the 'van tyres.

Do not leave the 'van on a soft, wet surface. If it must be parked in a field, run the wheels onto planks or bricks.

If you do not carry a spare wheel, make sure that your repair outfit is complete and that you have a set of tyre levers (get good tyre levers – it is well worth while). I think a spare wheel is a sound investment. You can make or buy a carrier which can be fitted out of the way under the 'van.

Spring Cleaning Your Motor Caravan

I am not concerned with the mechanical servicing of your 'van. This is all laid down in your instruction book for you to do yourself or as a matter for your garage. Let us look at the actual living quarters and driving cab of the vehicle. Although there are slight differences, most of the internal maintenance of the motor caravan applies to the trailer 'van.

The essential thing with the upholstery is to remove all traces of abrasive dust. You will be amazed how much sand and grit will accumulate in the seams and crevices. Work over the seats with a stiff brush and finish up with a vacuum cleaner.

You will find that sand and dust also get into the carpets. If possible, remove and clean them. Lino is easily cleaned by washing it and giving it a good going over with a polish containing a sealing agent. Again, dust and sand may get underneath. Remove the lino, if this is feasible, and brush the dust away.

Most working surfaces and the cooker are dealt with by wiping them over, but be sure to remove any grease which has splashed behind the cooker. Check the gas supply carefully. All taps and washers should receive attention, as should all joints in the gas supply. Check these with liquid soap, which will form bubbles if there is any leak.

Clean the water pump and any tank used to store your water supply. Window, drawer and door catches also require checking; if loose, they will rattle and, even worse, burst open and scatter your crockery and belongings all over the floor. Oil all catches lightly.

The rising roof should receive attention. Grease the runners, and examine the rubber seam strips on windows and skylights. Lubricate them with glycerine or, if necessary, renew them.

Finally, but most important, should your 'van have the engine inside the driving cab, always take care to cover the carpets and cushions while working on it; better still, take the upholstery and floor covering out altogether. Nothing spoils the appearance of a 'van more than oil or grease stains on the upholstery.

Part Four

Preparing for Your Holiday

Chapter 12

What Clothing Should You Take?
The Kit List

It does not matter what I say or what you intend, but one thing is certain – you will take too much clothing with you. Obviously, the type of clothing taken depends on where you are going; the wardrobe of the mountain camper will vary considerably from that of the camper or caravanner who pitches in the centre of Paris or the outskirts of Rome with the intention of touring these cities.

What is really required is something suitable for pitching a tent, erecting a trailer tent or stabilising a caravan in wet weather. I have done this wearing only a pair of swimming trunks, but most people prefer a little more than that. Also required is a comfortable outfit for walking (this may well be that which is used for pitching). Remember that heavy shoes, or preferably boots, are necessary for walking in the country. The ladies in particular should remember this. Very few of them, except established campers, own suitable shoes. Do not buy walking shoes or boots a few days before leaving; get them in plenty of time and wear them for short periods until they are broken in, otherwise they will break you in instead. There is great temptation to take best things "just in case". If you must visit restaurants which only admit customers wearing evening dress, that is what you will have to take. Most restaurants, however, including the best of them, are delighted to welcome anyone neatly dressed – so what more do you require? Ladies should bear in mind that at some resorts bikinis are not permitted.

Clothing takes up a considerable amount of space, so it must be reduced to a minimum without leaving you short or making you feel out of place on your holiday.

The Kit List

Gradually you will build up a kit list, a list of essential items which from experience has been reduced to a minimum. This is well worth while, for not only does it reduce the number of items which are taken along filling up valuable space and never used, but it also prevents essential things from being overlooked. Perhaps my family kit list will interest readers. In case you find it helpful, here it is:

1 *Clothing*. Gumboots, thick socks for boots or gumboots, rubber sandals (Judo type) for wet grass, shoes, boots, sandals (leather), handkerchiefs, socks, underclothing, shirts, heavy sweater, an anorak or windproof jersey, swimming trunks, canvas trousers for walking, a plastic mac, raincoat for use in town, pyjamas, track suit, hat or beret, and (for use in town) a jacket and tie.

2 *Personal kit*. Shoe cleaning kit, washing and shaving kit (including a mirror and a towel), sunglasses, address book.

3 *Documents*. Passport, driving licence, insurance certificate and Green Card, tickets, money and travellers cheques, maps and guides, camp site list, Camping Club membership card, R.A.C. or A.A. membership card, Camping Carnet.

4 *Camping equipment*. Tent (inner and outer tents in two separate bags), pegs, groundsheet for living space, small tent for boys (including groundsheet and pegs), plastic

sheet to go underneath the sewn-in groundsheet and separate groundsheet for living area, mallet, cooking table, chairs and stools, beds, torch, tent lamp, windbreak, sleeping bags, blankets, gas fire.

5 *Domestic.* Plastic bucket and basin, gas container (large), gas container (small), cooker (two-burner), cooker (single-burner), nest of cooking utensils, matches, water container, cutlery, crockery, egg cups, bread board and knife, tin opener, bottle opener, corkscrew, egg box, washing-up mop, dishcloth, insect repellent, frying pan (non-stick), pressure cooker, toilet paper, clothes line and pegs, sewing kit, washing-up powder, scouring powder, spare plastic bags, coat hangers, dustpan and brush, polyroll, thermos containers, kettle, containers for coffee, butter, meat, cooking fat, etc., potato peeler, strainer spoon, fish slice, scissors, milk bottle top and top for closing open tins, hot water bottle (for wife), paper tissues, water purifier tablets.

6 *Food.* Stock for the first day – in this I include coffee, milk (powder and evaporated), sugar, bread, butter, cooking fat, bacon, eggs, cheese, cereals, salt and pepper, drinks and cordials, packet soup, tinned fruit, tinned meat, tinned or dried vegetables, jam, marmalade, biscuits and powdered potato. You can add or subtract to this list as much as you like, but as I see it the main thing is to have sufficient stock in hand for the first day, especially if you start your holiday at a weekend. In addition, I take items of which only a small quantity are required, such as salt, pepper, mustard, etc., food which might be much more expensive if purchased locally, such as coffee bought abroad, and emergency rations for use if shops are closed or not available (powdered milk and food in tins).

7 *First-aid kit.* I think this should include Elastoplast, aspirin, thermometer, travel pills, anti-burn lotion, bandages, scissors, safety pins, waterproof and boil dressings, cotton wool, gauze and lint, T.C.P. or a similar antiseptic lotion, eye ointment or lotion, anti-sunburn cream and anti-sting lotion. You will add or subtract to this list from your own experience.

8 *Amusement.* Bats, rackets, balls and shuttles, field glasses, compass, reading and writing materials, camera, radio.

You will note that I have included neither tea nor a teapot. We never drink it, but don't overlook yours because it is omitted from my list. You may wish to include a latrine tent, closet, toilet fluid and a spade or entrenching tool; also liquid fuel for your cooker or heater should you use this type.

You will add all sorts of items to suit yourself. I have only attempted to give you an idea.

Chapter 13

Packing for the Journey

The Lightweight and Pedestrian Camper

The method of packing employed depends on the number of people in the party. The solo walker has to carry all his equipment himself and must pack accordingly, whereas two or three can use the same tent, which allows the various parts to be divided amongst them in the most appropriate way. As a rule, it is far more economic for a party of three or so to carry a tent of appropriate size between them than for each to take a small bivi tent. But, regardless of the number of walkers, one thing is inevitable: the kit will have to be carried on the back in a pack if you intend to travel any distance as opposed to a few miles in an odd weekend. It will pay you

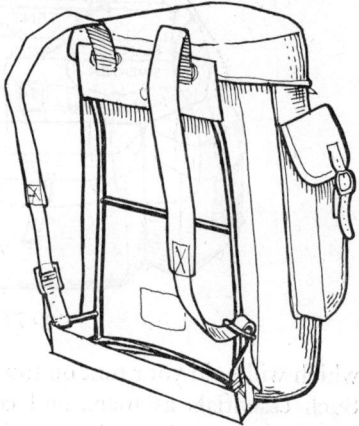

Fig. 70

to buy a good frame rucksack (see Fig. 70); they are fairly expensive, but they do permit you to carry a large load in comfort. I am not suggesting that you will be able to forget a loaded rucksack, but it will sit comfortably on your back, will not require constant hitching up and will leave your hands free.

Take great care to pack so that the items you will require first are on top (see Fig. 71). A good rucksack has straps

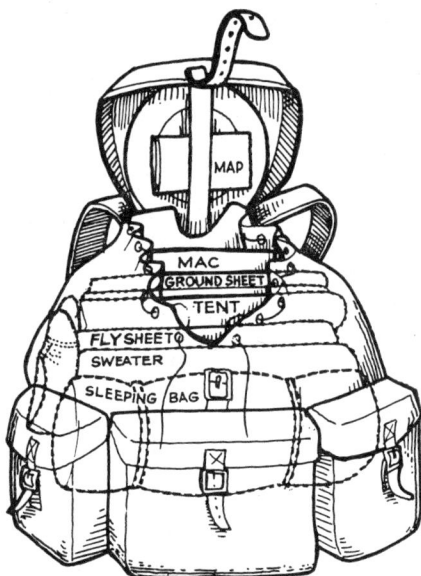

Fig. 71

which will hold your tent on top or at the back of the pack. Such essentials as maps and compass should be put in handy places in the rucksack or in your jacket pockets so as to be readily available. Pack so that nothing sways backwards or forwards – a water bottle banging against your hip can be infuriating. Your sleeping bag or blanket can also be strapped on top of your pack in a roll, providing that the weather is dry or you have a polythene bag to wrap it in. When you are packing your rucksack, keep the bulk of the weight high up so that it rests upon your shoulders rather than pressing in the small of your back (see Figs. 72 and 73).

Weight, of course, is important, but you will be surprised how much can be carried. For example, a small camping gas stove, cooking canteen, a small stool cup or mug and a couple of plates will not weigh more than 7 lbs if correctly chosen. A good tent such as the Black & Edgington "Good Companion Standard" with groundsheet will weigh only $5\frac{1}{2}$ lbs. This is a really roomy single poled tent.

Canned food is heavy, but there are many good dehydrated foods on the market. Soups and milk come to mind at once, and I have cooked some excellent powdered potato. Little plastic pots

Fig. 72

with airtight lids are most suitable for carrying butter, cooking fat, sugar, pepper and salt, etc. As regards eating implements, I think the little sets of cutlery are worth buying. If you take your knife, fork and spoon from home, you will continually be searching for one item at the bottom of your rucksack. The sets, however, always stay to-

gether, even if placed at the bottom of the rucksack – or they can go in a pocket.

Lighting can be by candle, although it is a little dangerous. Woolworths, however, sell a miniature oil lamp which is very suitable for lightweight campers, particularly if you use oil for cooking. Perhaps you turn in early and do not have this problem, and anyway I have already discussed the merits of various methods of lighting and cooking in Chapter 7.

What about tents? I have described the single pole type already. You can buy a continental ridge tent of the type called the Canadienne which sleeps three, or even four, people and weighs only 8 lbs; smaller ridge tents weigh even less. The choice must be yours in the end, but a visit to a good tent manufacturer such as Black & Edgington, who specialise in lightweight tents, is well worth while. Most camping exhibitions and showrooms concentrate on expensive frame tents which will not interest the lightweight camper. Fig. 74 shows a typical lightweight tent designed for severe conditions.

Fig. 73

Although personal kit should be kept to a minimum, it is better to take slightly too much rather than too little, which can result in cold, sleepless nights. Take extra socks for wet weather; putting on wet boots in the morning is not too bad as long as you have a dry pair of socks to wear with them. I think four pairs of socks are essential on a camping expedition. Try to buy pure woollen socks; these are absorbent and do not form hard lumps under your

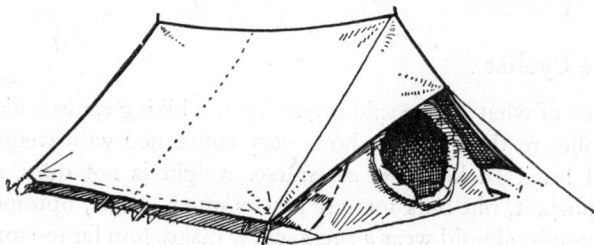

Fig. 74

feet. Do take a small shoe-cleaning outfit with you. Not only does it look awful to go into town with dirty shoes or boots but also a little polish – even on wet footwear – helps to keep the leather soft and comfortable.

Remember that it is unwise to buy a heavier pair of boots than necessary; every extra pound or two on your feet is the equivalent of some seven pounds on your back. It is better that your boots should be slightly too large and have to be worn with two pairs of socks than that they should be on the small side. Boots which fit nicely and are comfortable when you are walking unloaded tend to become too tight when you pick up your rucksack because the extra weight spreads your feet.

Whether you wear shorts or slacks (I personally dislike walking or scrambling in shorts), try to keep heavy and loose things out of your pockets. Also, try to avoid having to carry things in your hands – again, every extra pound or two carried in your hands or weighing down your arms is equivalent to an additional five pounds on your back.

Lightweight campers are more likely to suffer from exposure than their frame tent brethren. This is something which has to be watched and is extremely dangerous. It is discussed fully in Chapter 25.

The Cyclist

Most of what I have said regarding the hiking camper also applies to the cyclist, who is very concerned with weight and bulk. In his case, of course, weight is not quite so important, but bulk matters just as much. In my opinion, no cyclist should wear a rucksack; it makes him far too top-heavy and susceptible to wind pressure. The cyclist should pack his gear in pannier bags mounted on each side of his

Fig. 75

rear wheel. In addition, he can if he wishes carry an extra bag on a carrier mounted on his rear mudguard. It is very important that he fits these panniers correctly as any sideways swing can be dangerous (see Fig. 75).

Let us have a look at a kit list used by an acquaintance of mine: tent $5\frac{1}{2}$ lbs, sleeping bag $3\frac{1}{2}$ lbs, track-suit 2 lbs, clothes 6 lbs, cooking canteen, eating equipment and stool $5\frac{1}{2}$ lbs, Camping Gaz stove $4\frac{1}{2}$ lbs, waterproof cycling suit $4\frac{1}{2}$ lbs – total $31\frac{1}{2}$ lbs. To this add a small first-aid kit, maps, gloves for cycling and a camera. The track suit doubles as a spare outfit and pyjamas, whilst the clothes include a spare pair of slacks and a sweater.

Incidentally, when I speak of pannier bags, a pair of ex-Forces packs purchased from a surplus store will do fine; a good and useful job can also be made from aluminium.

The Motor Cyclist and Scooter Rider

A camper using this form of transport has the same problems of keeping his kit to a minimum bulk as the hiker and cyclist, but, according to the power of his machine, he has far less worry about weight. In fact, he is able to carry as much weight as the limit of space allows. I do not feel so strongly about the wearing of a rucksack in the case of the motorised camper as he is not quite so much at the mercy of the wind and, riding a heavy and powerful machine, is not so top-heavy with the weight on his back. He will use the same type of tent as the other lightweight enthusiasts, but is able to take a larger one and more ambitious equipment.

I had a word with a young friend who uses a Lambretta for camping, taking a friend on his pillion, and he provided me with the following details. He uses two ex-army packs, one on each side of the rear wheel; he also has a strong carrier on the rear mudguard. Each uses one pack, into which they place their personal gear such as clothing. A collapsible water carrier and a collapsible wash bowl are packed on the rear carrier, with two sleeping bags rolled up, two blankets and two air beds placed on top. These are covered with a waterproof sheet, which is used to cover the scooter when in camp. A second carrier is fixed above the front wheel, and in this is placed the tent (they use a Canadienne) and the eating and cooking equipment. If required, the pillion passenger wears an additional small pack, which is adjusted to rest on top of the rolled-up sleeping bags and blankets. This takes the weight and avoids any danger of the passenger losing her balance backwards. I told my friend that I thought he was top-heavy and too susceptible to wind, but he replied that all the real weight is placed low down in the panniers and, in any case, they had travelled all over Europe without mis-hap – I still think they were overloaded!

The Motorist

Here we come to the "weight and bulk no object" luxury camper – the type of vehicle he uses and the number of passengers he takes dictating how near he approaches first-class hotel standards when on the site. There are varying opinions on how to pack a car. The general rule is to keep the weight between the axles, but this is not easy with a modern car as most have huge boots extending well beyond the back axle. You will read that it is very unwise to use a roof rack, since this provides the wind with something substantial to push at and upsets the balance of the car, and you may be advised to use a luggage trailer. There are

many very good ones on the market at reasonable prices, or
they can be hired. Before deciding to tow a trailer, remember that the speed limit in the United Kingdom for any
form of two-wheel trailer is 40 miles an hour; but there are
other restrictions, so I advise you to check up on this. As I
have said, opinions differ and I am only offering my own
ideas – ideas which are based on many years' experience.
In fact, the object of this book is not to lay down the law
on camping, but rather to help the inexperienced camper
and to exchange ideas with the "experts".

The first principle of packing the car is "last in – first
out". If you want a hot drink when you stop on the way,
either have your stove and picnic outfit in the car or pack
it last so that it will be on top. Our car is fairly large, so
"wanted on voyage" gear is kept inside the car, either by
the front passenger's feet or on the transmission tunnel
between the rear seat passengers. The use of thermos
flasks avoids having to heat your drink en route, but there
is always the danger that these will get broken rolling
about the car or knocking about the tent. We usually carry
cold drinks in bottles and hot soup in the flasks; if need be,
we can heat a drink on the small single-burner Camping
Gaz stove which we keep as a spare in case the big one runs
out at an inconvenient moment. We also consume a large
number of boiled sweets on the journey.

On arrival the first job is, of course, to pitch the tent.
This must be done quickly, especially in wet weather –
even if it is dry, it is still a chore and better finished as soon
as possible. For this reason, the tent must be packed away
so that it is quickly available in the boot or on the roof.
Most of my camping has been done with a series of Ford
cars and my experience has resulted in an effort to keep
down the weight in the boot as far as possible. Our tent

therefore goes on the roof rack as close to the front as possible and, as a result, my car continues to handle well and I
do not find my headlamps pointing upwards to infuriate
other drivers. This is important, because once your vehicle
becomes tail heavy your headlamps will cause dazzle and
all approaching motorists will give you a dose of full beam
in reply. With the weight on the roof I have to watch roll
on corners and, of course, the effects of unwise braking at
corners are emphasised. Naturally, when using a roof rack,
whatever luggage is placed on top adds to the car's wind
resistance. A typical well-covered roof rack is shown in
Fig. 76. Returning to my original point, if the tent is

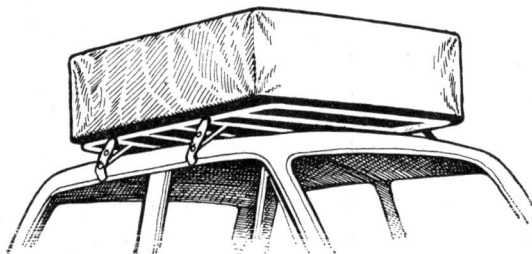

Fig. 76

available immediately you stop, you can put up the frame
and throw the fabric over it within a few seconds, which is
most important in bad weather.

To the family man off on a two or three weeks' holiday a
roof rack or trailer is essential. To attempt to talk your wife
into reducing her kit is to risk divorce. We avoid using
firm-sided suitcases as these restrict packing arrangements;
soft hold-alls and cardboard boxes in the boot are far more
convenient. Of course, your wife will require one suitcase
to pack dresses, etc., which must be folded in a certain way.

When we put our heavy frame tent on the roof, the remainder of the gear up there must be light. I use the rest of the space for two canvas hold-alls, containing clothes and a couple of sleeping bags in their waterproof covers. All the gear on the roof goes into a zip cover, which is also waterproof, and the whole arrangement is held secure by a rubber, octopus-type strap.

At the front end of the boot we push our camp beds and heavy items, such as our gas containers. On one side there is the plastic bucket, used for washing up but which en route holds all the crockery and cutlery, the cooking utensils and water container (2-gallon plastic). On the other side, behind the spare wheel, go all the shoes and gumboots – loose to fit in better. The middle then takes three boxes of clothes, the cooking table and chairs, folded flat, and the cooker. On top of this lot we put our coats. The other sleeping bags and blankets are spread out along the bench seat in the back of the car and sat on, whilst the table on which we eat is tied to the back of the driver's seat.

Incidentally, remember to check the roof rack itself after a few miles; it may have settled down and need tightening up. Should you use cord to tie your gear securely to your roof rack, check this also after a few miles. As the kit on the rack settles down, the cord will require tightening. I use a well-tailored cover which goes all round my kit, even underneath, closing with a zip, but if you do not have such a cover a waterproof sheet, which can be used in camp, is useful. Make sure it will hold everything securely; it is embarrassing to drive along shedding odds and ends – and, believe me, I've done it.

If you propose to stop on the way at a hotel or to spend a night in the cabin of a cross-Channel boat, it is worth remembering that you will require sleeping, washing and shaving kit, and you should pack to allow this to be reached without the necessity of a major upheaval.

Finally, remember that it is illegal to overload a vehicle with passengers or goods to the extent that danger is caused to the occupants of your car or to any other person. Should you have an accident in an overloaded car, you are

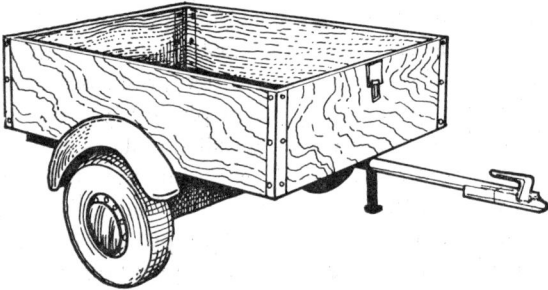

Fig. 77

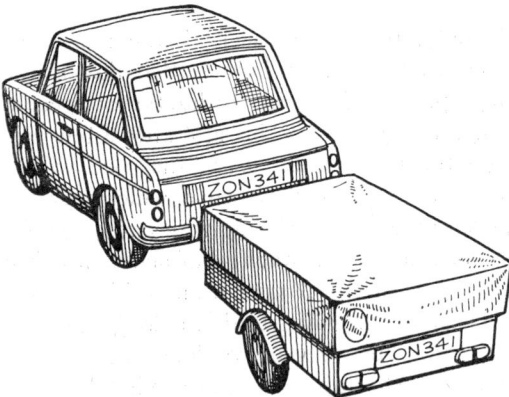

Fig. 78

likely to find yourself in serious and very expensive trouble.

Packing a Luggage Trailer

This does not provide any great problem. The object is to place the weight over the wheels so that the trailer is evenly balanced when loaded (see Figs. 77 and 78). Having the bulk of the weight forward or at the rear causes trouble with the road-holding of the car, just as does placing too

Fig. 79

much weight in the boot or at the front of the car itself. In addition, remember that the trailer has to be disconnected from the car and manhandled; if the weight is nicely balanced over the wheels this will be quite easy. Some trailers can be disconnected from the chassis and used as a set of shelves (see Fig. 79).

Chapter 14

Preparing the Car

You must consider your car when planning a camping holiday. For the most part of the year, the majority of cars carry only one or two people for comparatively short distances; then, in the heat of summer, four people climb in, every inch of space – including that on the roof rack – being packed with luggage, and the car is expected to run non-stop and flat out for about three hundred miles. Perhaps you do not pack your car with equipment, but instead tow a caravan or luggage trailer. This will still place a strain on the car to which it is not accustomed. As a result, breakdowns are likely to occur at weak points. The parts of the car which take most of the strain are:

1. The springs.
2. The tyres.
3. The cooling system.
4. The brakes.
5. The steering.
6. The battery.

The surprising thing is not that there are so many breakdowns but rather that so many people get away with it. My experience is that breakdowns are most likely to occur with new cars or those that have done over 50 000 miles. You get teething troubles at first, but after about 3000 miles your vehicle has settled down and all the weaknesses have received attention. I would certainly not go very far from a good main agent whilst on a family holiday with a car that was not fully run in. On the other hand, as the car gets older it has to be coddled. However, it is not the age of the car that counts, but the condition in which it is kept. I have seen Austin Sevens and Morris Eights (real ones, not the front wheel drive variety) all over Europe, but have never seen one broken down. This is because the owners care enthusiastically for them. The broken-down cars I have seen have been the "taken for granted" modern ones.

Let us now look at the parts of the car which take most of the stress one at a time.

1 *The springs*

These weaken with age and, whilst a broken spring is rare, the unusual load forces them down, with the result that the vital parts beneath the car are far more likely to hit rocks on the road and the car will bottom unpleasantly on bumps. You can buy good, cheap spring assisters which are easy to fit even if you are only a very average handyman. If you are towing, it will probably pay you to fit these in any case. Should a spring leaf be broken, it must, of course, be replaced.

2 *The tyres*

The tyres are just common sense; you always need good tyres, but to drive fast for long distances carrying a heavy load, which includes your family, with doubtful tyres is insane. See that the walls are unbroken and that you have plenty of tread. A crack in a side wall can result in a burst as the tyre heats up. Check for bulges in the side wall (inside as well as out), especially in tubeless tyres. For long distance driving, it is usual to raise the tyre pressure by a few pounds, and when you carry a full load as well I would suggest an increase in pressure of about 4 lbs to 6 lbs (your garage can advise you on this). Do not forget the spare. Some continental countries have strict laws regarding worn or faulty tyres which are firmly enforced. Even if you have tubeless tyres, it is sensible to take a spare inner tube.

3 *The cooling system*

A common problem is over-heating. An engine runs best at a little below boiling point; it is happy hot and even a really clogged-up cooling system will operate satisfactorily at home on short runs with no load. A full load is another matter, however, and when faced with a long haul over the Alps you will soon find your vision blocked by clouds of steam. Before leaving, check all the water hoses and their connections; they are particularly likely to leak at the ends where they are held by the clips. Should the hose be long enough, you can cure this by cutting about a quarter or half an inch off the end, but you will usually find that you have to buy a new radiator hose. Empty the radiator and re-fill it with hot water, pouring in a little of one of the proprietary radiator flushing fluids. This will produce a load of sludge, and when it has been emptied you should wash out the radiator once more. A flushing fluid will find any leaks or weak spots, so you should not leave this job until the day before you leave. Check that your fan belt is in good condition and sufficiently tight; it is a vital part of the cooling system. If it begins to slip or gets broken, you will find yourself short of electricity.

4 *The brakes*

Your brakes must be in good trim. They should be included in the general servicing of your car, but I always insist that they receive special attention before I go on holiday. Ensure that there is plenty of brake lining left and then adjust. After adjustment, see that all the wheels revolve freely when the brakes are off. Remember that disc brakes are designed to be in permanent light contact.

5 *The steering*
There should be about an inch of free play on the steering; any more than that shows that there is wear somewhere. Overall wear through use will be inevitable as the car ages, but you or your garage should ensure that the vehicle is safe. Wear tends not to be obvious from the handling of the car because you become used to it and adjust yourself to the effects (the same applies to worn brakes – you drive accordingly and all goes well until an emergency occurs). However, maladjustment usually shows itself in uneven wear of the tyres and peculiar handling.

6 *The battery*
It is fatal to chance a dicey battery on holiday. I know that long runs give a very good charge, but your car will be parked on grass at the site and exposed to damp and condensation. This can make it hard to start your car and really give your battery a bashing. You can obtain waterproof sprays which protect the electrics from damp, and it always helps to spread an old towel or piece of blanket over the top of the engine at night when you are parked on your site (the blanket goes under the bonnet, of course).

All the above items should be carefully checked before leaving home. In addition, it may well pay you to have your headlamps adjusted to allow for the weight in the boot. Your garage can do this for you quite easily.

If you do not service your car yourself, have it given the full treatment at the garage – a 5000-mile service. This will include checking the wheel bearings, tuning and so on. I consider it very unwise to have your car serviced only a day or two before you leave home because any faults in the garage's work will reveal themselves during your trip. On the other hand, if you allow yourself time to drive quite a few miles after servicing, any problems will show up and can be adjusted prior to setting off. I well remember the comments of a friend who collected his car from the garage the night before he left home and was forced to drive across Europe on wet roads with brakes which pulled hard to the right. He was very fortunate and made it safely, but had he failed to do so would only have had himself to blame.

What Size Trailer Can You Expect Your Car to Tow?

Cars vary in towing ability, so it is best to obtain the manufacturer's views on the weight your particular model may reasonably be expected to handle. The following figures, however, which have been supplied by the manufacturers of some of the more popular models at the time of writing, will serve to give you an idea of the amount of weight your car is capable of pulling:

B.L.M.C. 1800	17 cwts
B.L.M.C. 1300	15 cwts
B.L.M.C. Mini	8 cwts
Cortina	16 cwts
Minx	17 cwts
Viva	15 cwts
V.W.	$12\frac{1}{2}$ cwts
Zephyr Six	$23\frac{1}{2}$ cwts

Remember that your warranty may well be void if you tow a heavier 'van than that laid down by the manufacturer.

At the present time, however, regulations are proposed which will set a weight limit for caravans. These state that the maximum gross weight of the caravan (which will be indicated on a plate fitted to the 'van) must not be more than the kerbside weight of the car. This is the weight usually given in the car's handbook and includes fuel, tools, spare wheel, etc., but not the passengers or luggage. Trailers fitted with power-operated brakes will be exempt from this rule.

Modern caravans tow easily. In 1967 a Sprite 'van was towed round Bryanston Square in London by two girls riding a tandem. This was not intended very seriously, but it does show that a well-balanced 'van can be towed by a small car.

Car Sickness

A great deal has been said, and written, about car sickness, so I will keep my comments short. "Experts" tell me that the chief causes of this are the floating movement of the modern car produced by its soft suspension and sideways rolling which, I suppose, is mainly due to thoughtless or sheer bad driving. This is supported by the fact that rear seat passengers are more inclined to suffer from car sickness. However, some people who should know say that the cause is primarily nerves and excitement. Certainly children suffer most and they nearly all grow out of it.

There are many suggestions put forward to prevent or cure this malady, such as "static" chains dangling from the car to earth static electricity. But these chains only work, if they do work at all, by a sort of black magic; there is no scientific foundation for supposing that they can prevent sickness. The best prevention is to drive smoothly and avoid roll or jerky progress. You should not allow children to read or look at books in the car and, if possible, stop them looking at anything that flashes by very close to the vehicle. Do not give them cakes or sweets, although they may suck boiled sweets. Should the whole family suffer from sickness, it might be as well to have the car's suspension and exhaust system checked.

Buying a New Car?

When buying a new car, the camper naturally takes into consideration his holiday requirements. But to what extent anyone who would normally find a Mini satisfactory should buy a large car merely in order to be able to carry substantial camping gear for about three weeks in a year is a matter of opinion.

I am told that the obvious solution is to decide on your car without any thought of your holiday and then buy the estate car version of it. Unfortunately, these cost about £100 more than the basic version and some look as if the additional section has been welded on the back of the car as an afterthought. Another snag is that if you have to use the back seats for passengers, as most of us do on holiday, you are left with the same floor area for luggage as you would have had in the boot of the car version. You can, of course, carry considerably more luggage by loading up to the roof, but if you do this you will completely block your vision in the rear view mirror. Even with wing mirrors, I feel very unhappy when I cannot see through the back window. I thought I had decided on an estate car, but having had a good look at them changed my mind. If you do buy an estate model, watch your insurance and taxation position. If you use it to carry your personal gear, private insurance and tax are sufficient, but do not be tempted to carry trade goods. Incidentally, all my friends who run estate cars complain that the rear door rattles or is draughty – or both.

Perhaps I have been unfair to the estate car. If you do buy one, I am sure you will find that you have a first-class vehicle. In some models the seats are so arranged that they can be converted into a double bed – or at least it is usually possible to sleep on air beds on the luggage platform with the seats folded back – and you do have a vehicle with a suspension which is built to take the heavy load you require. The estate car will handle far better when heavily laden than will the standard car.

When you have chosen your car, you have a further decision to make – should you have automatic transmission? With it you will find town driving much more pleasant, but above all it is ideal for the camper. As it keeps the engine pulling at its most effective, you will find it a great advantage in carrying heavy loads and towing a trailer or caravan. It also enables you to climb the long gradients found on the Continent in a higher gear and in a silence which is very impressive. Automatic transmission is now fitted to estate cars and even to motor caravans.

Chapter 15

Preparing to Tow Your Caravan

Before you can tow a 'van you will have to have your car fitted up with a towing bracket (see Fig. 80). Although modern British and continental 'vans have standard towing arrangements and electric connections, it is a good idea to obtain full details of your 'van's towing arrangements from the dealer. Modern car fittings are well developed and neat, and are no eyesore when fitted. Towing brackets are made specially for individual makes of car and can be fitted without too much difficulty by a good handyman. Unless you can handle tools, however, I advise you to get your garage to fit the bracket and lighting equipment. It is as well to remember that the labour charges will approximately equal or even exceed the cost of the fitting. The standard ball size is now 50 mm, which in Britain has replaced the old 2-inch model. The difference appears to be practically nil, but from the engineering point of view it is considerable. Do not attempt to connect a 2-inch ball with a 50-mm fitting, or a 50-mm ball with a 2-inch fitting. This can result in disaster.

Fig. 80

Having arranged to link the 'van securely to your car, you now have to look to the electrical side. The law is strict and has to be complied with in all respects, and I am sure you will wish to be safe on the road, even if only for your own sake. For example, it is necessary to have the 'van fitted with tail and stop lights, the number plate has to be illuminated, and you must have left and right turn indicators. Incidentally, should the 'van be much wider than your car, it will also be necessary to have white lights on the front of the 'van. Nowadays, a seven-pin plug is standard and your 'van is almost certain to be equipped with such a fitting. You should ensure that you have your car fitted up in the same way.

Towing for the First Time

Now your caravan is ready to be linked up with the car. It is complete with lights, number plate and so on. If you are anything like me, tension will grow as the time of your first tow approaches until you are verging on blind panic. This is not necessary. My first experience of towing was being ordered into an army Land Rover with a large loaded water-tank trailer hooked onto the back and having to drive it some sixty miles along busy main roads and narrow country lanes. I was amazed how easy it was, with the exception of backing. This is a different story and I will discuss it later. I do not wish to give the impression that anyone can climb into a car with a caravan on the back and drive off without a thought – this could be dangerous. But if you take it carefully and easily you will find that most of the anticipated problems do not exist.

Some caravan dealers will provide a free driving lesson without additional charge and this is well worth taking into consideration if you are without any experience of towing. You drive your car into the dealer's yard and there is your 'van waiting for you. Remember that it is easier to sit in your car and to drive your towing bracket up to the drawbar of the 'van (see Fig. 81) than it is to push or pull

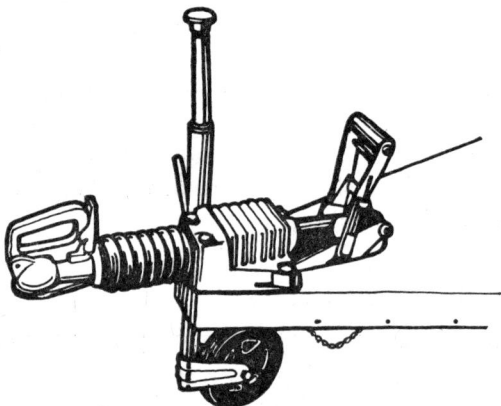

Fig. 81

the 'van up to the car. First, however, you must get out of the car and walk over to the 'van. Raise the front suffici-ently high for the ball on the car to slip underneath by means of the screw adjustable jockey wheel on the 'van. At first it will pay you to have an assistant to guide you whilst you back into position. Later you may be able to do this alone. If you do have an assistant, please ensure that both you and he (or she) understand the signals, whether by voice or by hand. This not only saves time but, as your assistant will usually be your wife, will also avoid a family row. Remember that it is easier to push the front of the 'van a little sideways than backwards or forwards, so it is important to judge your distance from the 'van accurately.

The 'van is heavy, so never attempt to lift it should the drawbar be too low for the ball. This is a certain means of injuring your back and spoiling your holiday. If, when fully extended, the jockey wheel is still too low, let down the front corner supports of the 'van to take the weight. This permits you to retract the jockey wheel, adjust it and re-lock it in a higher position. The dealer should demonstrate all this to you. The coupling usually closes with a definite click, so you will be able to know when it is secure. The jockey wheel is shown folded back in Fig. 81.

You are now hitched up and ready to go. If you stand back and look at your outfit, you will be horrified to find that you are faced with driving something as long as a motor coach and, as far as the 'van is concerned, considerably higher. In addition, your outfit has a hinge in the middle, which makes it easier than a coach to drive forwards but far more difficult to reverse. Before driving off, there are a few checks to make:

1. First, ensure that you are securely hitched up.
2. Next, by releasing your hand-brake, get an assistant to check that the brake lights, flashing indicators and tail lamps on the 'van work.
3. At the same time, ensure that nothing has obstructed your caravan brake if it is of the overrun type. Should the brake be blocked it cannot operate.
4. You can obtain wing mirrors with extending arms for your car. These are very useful, as they ensure good vision when towing but can be pushed into the normal position when driving the car on its own. Should you have poor vision or none at all through the 'van from your internal mirror, you might consider it worth while to fit one of the periscope

arrangements which fix on the roof of your car to provide a view through the windows of the 'van. These are quickly removed when you are not towing. Whatever method you use to obtain a view to the rear, ensure that it is adjusted correctly.

5. Check that the stabilising legs of the 'van and the jockey wheel are raised and secured.

Now you can stand back and have a look at the trim of your outfit. It should ride level or, at the most, a little nose down (see Fig. 82). If necessary, adjust the balance by moving the weight of your stores in the 'van. If your car has soft springing, you may have stacked too much in the boot and may well require some form of spring assister.

At this stage you are ready to drive off, but again you have several points to remember:

A. The 'van is wider than your car – it may be considerably wider. If you are one of those drivers who pride themselves on being able to drive through a gap without slowing down provided you have two inches to spare on each side of the car, you are liable to get a nasty and expensive shock. I am aware that to know and to be able to judge the width of your car is one of the hallmarks of a good driver, but this will not stop a nasty crunching noise if you forget the extra width of your caravan.

B. You are now driving a long vehicle – 30 ft is not exceptional. This means that, should you take a corner fairly close to the kerb in your car, the inside wheels of your 'van will run over the pavement. Even if you do not hit a pedestrian or lamp-post, this can damage the tyre and even the suspension of the 'van. Remember also that you must give an over-

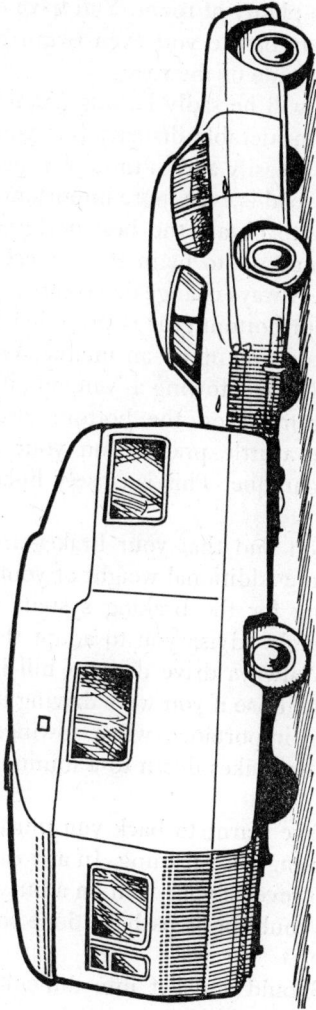

Fig. 82

taken vehicle plenty of room. You have to draw the 'van well clear before you even begin to cut back towards the inside of the road.

C. Acceleration will be sadly lacking. At first this will cause you considerable dismay, but you will soon learn to take it easily and to time your gear changes. Reading the road is even more important when towing in order to obtain the best performance from your car. You have to be in the correct gear at the correct time. Always change down early when climbing hills. Your bottom gear is provided for driving, not just for starting up on an incline. You may well have to use it when towing a 'van, and if you do not have synchromesh on the bottom gear you had better get in a little practice on your double declutching technique. This is closely linked with my next point.

D. You will soon find that your brakes are adversely affected by the additional weight of your 'van, even after allowing for the braking system of the 'van itself. I strongly advise you to adopt the old army principle – "always drive down a hill in the same gear you would use if you were driving up". This is of particular importance when towing. Keep the strain on your brakes down to a minimum and use your gears.

E. Until you have learnt to back you must be careful to avoid missing your turning. In any case, you will be unable to reverse your 'van on a busy road, even though you could perhaps have done so with a car on its own.

F. Warning! Should you get into difficulty on a hill never – *never* – unhitch.

G. Despite a popular belief to the contrary, it is not illegal to carry passengers in the 'van whilst towing, but my advice is, do not do so. The windows are unlikely to be made of safety glass and in the case of an accident can cause terrible injuries; also, should the driver brake hard, anyone in the 'van can be hurled from one end of it to the other.

H. Remember that there is a maximum speed limit of 40 miles per hour in the United Kingdom. This includes motorway driving. On motorways, trailer outfits are not allowed in the fast lane of three-lane carriageways.

Reversing and Driving Tips

As long as you take it easy, towing a caravan is fairly straightforward and presents few problems to the average driver. By far the greatest of these problems is that of reversing. If you start with your outfit in a straight line and reverse the car to the left, the 'van will turn right – possibly with expensive results. Once you understand the reason for this you only require practice. I have tried to make the principle of reversing simple with a series of diagrams. To obtain the necessary practice find a *very* quiet road or, even better, a quiet corner of a camp site. Driving practice is quite rightly frowned upon on sites, but if you join the Caravan Club and attend one of their social weekends you will easily find someone to help you if you have a word with the Steward.

Start with the outfit lined up – i.e. with your car and 'van in a straight line. Now, in theory, if you reverse very slowly, the outfit will move back without deviating to left or right. In fact, of course, the camber of the road, uneven

ground or a slight deviation from a straight line when lining up the 'van will slowly swing the 'van one way or
another. For the purpose of this lesson, however, ignore
this and assume that you are perfectly lined up on level
ground. Fig. 83 shows the outfit in a straight line, and from

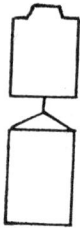
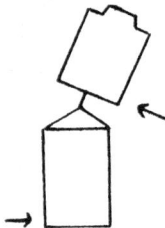

Fig. 83   *Fig. 84*   *Fig. 85*

this position you pull left-hand down on the steering
wheel. As you do so, the back of the car turns left, exerting
pressure on the 'van's drawbar in the same direction. As a
result, the 'van pivots on its wheels and swings to the
right. These movements are shown with arrows in Fig. 84.
If you go on driving, your 'van will continue in the same
direction until the rear corner of the car meets the corner
of the 'van (see Fig. 85). This is known as 'jack-knifing'
and can cause considerable damage.

    This experiment should have provided the key to revers-
ing the trailer. Go back to Fig. 83. You wish to reverse
to the left, but this time you turn your wheels round
to the right (right-hand down). Start to drive backwards
very slowly. Your car will turn to the right, pushing the
drawbar in the same direction. As a result, the 'van pivots
on its wheels and begins to turn left, which is the desired
direction (see Fig. 86). Immediately straighten up and

begin to turn the car wheels left so that it follows the 'van round to the left, the whole outfit moving exactly where you want it to go (see Fig. 87). Incidentally, driving backwards in a straight line is far more difficult than it appears because the slightest pressure to left or right on the draw-

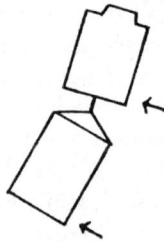

Fig. 86   Fig. 87

bar will immediately pivot the 'van on its wheels so that the trailer turns quite sharply, although the car has only turned a very gentle curve.

Should you overshoot the desired turning, think twice before making a "U" turn. If you turn too sharply your outfit will "jack-knife", thus causing a monumental traffic jam. If you really must make such a turn, ensure that you have sufficient room to complete it without backing. If, as is quite likely to happen the first time, you do misjudge it, straighten up for the last few yards in order to line up the outfit so that you can avoid a "jack-knife". Now you will be able to reverse your lock as you back and succeed in your turn on the second attempt.

If you are forced to come to a stop on a hill, you may find yourself unable to get started again. This is not because your car is unable to pull such a weight up the hill – it can. The problem is the clutch, which cannot take the load. Your engine produces little torque at low revs, and an uphill start requires severe and damaging slipping of the clutch. The answer is to wait for a gap in the traffic and then back gently, running the nearside wheel of the 'van at an angle back against the kerb. Now you will be able to get the car started whilst the 'van is turning and this is sufficient to get the whole outfit going. Should you get to the foot of a steep hill, you may think it worth stopping if you find yourself behind a heavily laden lorry or a bus which is obviously going to stop in order to give yourself a clear run. I repeat – when you come to a stop on a hill *never* unhitch.

A trouble which you are likely to run into is mud on the camping site. Immediately a driving wheel on the car begins to spin, stop. If you continue, you will rapidly dig yourself deep into the mud. If you are already moving across the field at a reasonable speed, it is, of course, silly to stop. In this case, ease off on the accelerator as soon as your wheels start to spin and attempt to keep going with as little power as possible. Once you come to a stop, you must declutch to avoid digging holes under the driving wheels. At a site, no doubt you will soon have all the volunteers you require to push you clear, but should you be alone pack sacks, stones, twigs or pieces of wood under the wheels to give them purchase. Don't forget to return to clean up the mess as soon as you are clear. I have heard people advised to unhitch, drive the car onto firm ground and pull the 'van out with a rope from car to 'van. My advice is, don't try it. When you unhitch the 'van, you have to lower the jockey wheel to balance it and this immediately digs itself into the soft ground, stopping the tow.

One final point on driving – it is easier to back a 'van round to the right than to the left. This is because you

have better vision in this direction, especially if you open
the offside door and lean out.

Towing Troubles – and What To Do

Many of the troubles which arise when towing are caused
by nothing more than inexperience. A new caravanner may
find his outfit unstable at 30 miles per hour, whilst an experienced man can drive the same outfit over the same
road at 60 miles per hour quite smoothly. You must take
it easy as you gain experience. The two main problems
which arise whilst you are towing are "pitching" and
"snaking".

Pitching
This is an up and down movement of the nose of the caravan. It also affects the car in the same way and is most unpleasant to the passengers. It can have several causes,
which include weak rear springing on the towing vehicle, a
faulty towing fixture on the car and a badly loaded caravan. Never skimp on the car's towing fixture, as it has to
take severe stress. Several manufacturers make special
brackets to fit most makes of cars. As there is no standard
height for 'van or trailer drawbars, it is important to fix
the towing fixture at the correct height for the particular
outfit. I advise fitting by experts. In any case, the 'van
should ride level or very slightly nose down at the most. To
tow a 'van which does not ride level can cause both pitching and snaking. If you have a car with a long overhanging
boot or with soft springing, the back of the car will sink
when you hitch up, thus taking the weight off the front
wheels and causing steering problems. There are several
solutions to this soft springing problem. I advise a word
with your dealer.

Snaking

This is far more dangerous than pitching. Sometimes the rear of the caravan can swing from side to side without altering the course of the car. When this happens it is called "tail-wagging". Should this go a stage further and throw the car from side to side, it is called snaking and can be caused by loading the 'van badly. A typical example of bad loading is placing heavy tins of food or water or gas containers too high up in the 'van. Other causes are worn suspension on the car or 'van, under or unevenly inflated tyres, worn steering on the car, or bad driving, such as a sudden swerve caused by cutting in too sharply when overtaking. A far less likely cause, unless you have a very old 'van, is faulty design of the caravan itself.

The tendency when experiencing snaking for the first time is to steer the opposite way to correct the movement. This, however, only makes the trouble worse. The answer is gentle acceleration in order to pull the 'van straight or very gentle braking.

A good 'van, a properly selected and fixed towing bracket on the car, and correct loading prevent these troubles, but you may consider it worth while to invest in a stabilising device. There are several good and effective ones about. Again, I suggest seeking advice from your dealer.

Shunting

This is caused by weak springs on the overrun brakes fitted to the caravan. Each time you slow, the 'van brake is applied with an effect similar to that produced by the buffers on a shunting train – a series of jerks. The answer is a new spring, if available, or a replacement unit.

Towing at Speed

Again, I must point out that the legal speed limit in this country is 40 miles per hour – even on motorways. All your high speed touring must be done abroad. As you become more experienced you will find it difficult not to gradually build up speed when travelling hundreds of miles along European motorways, so if you intend to go abroad you must consider high speed work.

Obviously, continental high speed places far greater strains and stresses on the outfit than those caused by comparatively low speeds at home. It is clear, therefore, that the outfit must be in first-class condition. A common trouble resulting from continued high speed is the seizing up of the wheel bearings, and special care is required in this respect. Tyres also give trouble. Maintain the pressures recommended by the manufacturer and do not forget that the car's rear tyres should be given about 5 lbs more pressure than when it is being driven without the 'van.

Special attention must be paid to the loading of the 'van. Equipment and personal gear must be stored as low down and as close to the axle as possible. I advise some experimenting with your loading and careful driving until you get it to your satisfaction. You cannot tow an unstable 'van at speed. In fact, it will be dangerous on the road even at slow speeds.

Take care when meeting cross winds. 'Vans have been blown completely over, and particular care must be exercised when leaving a stretch sheltered by, say, trees or buildings. It is easy to overlook the wind and find oneself in difficulty. A cross wind, particularly if blowing diagonally from the rear, can cause snaking. Cobbled roads, especially when wet, demand careful driving.

All the points I have made about normal touring, such as using the gears to reduce speed, careful overtaking, no sudden movements of the steering wheel, etc., are even more important when towing fast.

It is unreasonable to expect a 'van which has stood in the open all the year and only received a little attention prior to a holiday to be in condition for a fast run along a motorway. The drawbar, wheel bearings, brakes and tyres all require checking, and I advise that this is done by experts. Tyres in particular deteriorate. Unless you have matching wheels and tyres on car and 'van, you may consider it wise to obtain and carry a spare for the caravan itself.

Chapter 16

Camping in Europe

Holidaying in Europe is no problem nowadays. It is not very many years since obtaining and completing all the forms was an adventure in itself, and watching your car sway up into the air with a hook under each wheel as it was transferred from the dock to the ship was a terrifying experience. All this has changed. Forms have been reduced to a minimum and are easily obtainable. On arrival at the docks, the car, motor caravan, or car and trailer is safely driven onto the boat through high doors at the end. Travel by air is just as simple.

I suppose more people are put off a continental holiday by the thought of driving on the right than by any other reason, such as foreign money or obtaining documents. But, as long as you take it easily, you will be amazed how quickly you settle down to driving on the "wrong side". In fact, it is changing back when you return home which is tricky. I have turned right onto the right-hand side to the surprise of a bus driver and taken a roundabout the wrong way immediately after landing in England. The secret is simply to take it carefully.

I appear to have started this chapter in the middle. First, you have to prepare the vehicle and arrange to take the car overseas.

Preparing Your Car

There is nothing special about this. The loading and pre-holiday servicing of the car are exactly the same as if you were travelling at home, and have already been discussed in Chapters 13 and 14 respectively.

However, if you are one of those people who chase the sun, hoping to get hotter and more settled weather by going south, you should bear in mind that your car is likely to receive a particularly heavy hammering. Remember, too, that not only will you be travelling farther and perhaps faster than your car is used to but that, in many cases, you will also encounter inferior and much more hilly roads. As you travel farther afield, especially to East Europe, you will find that the roads become steadily worse off the motorways; you may even meet unmetalled roads in places. Although it is fair to say that, with the exception of mountain areas, hills in Europe are not much steeper than those in the United Kingdom, they do tend to be miles, as opposed to yards, long. Thus your car must receive a very thorough servicing prior to setting off – even more so than when holidaying at home, as a breakdown abroad may be difficult to put right, particularly if you are visiting an out-of-the-way place or have an unusual make of vehicle.

There are a few further points to consider when preparing to take your car abroad.

1 *Lights*

At home, the police do not bother a motorist who has only one side-light or brake-light working, although strictly this is illegal and also highly dangerous. On the Continent, however, an on-the-spot fine will quite rightly result.

Check your lights, therefore, and replace any defective bulbs. As your lamps will throw a beam full in the face of a driver coming the opposite way, it is essential to get your headlamps converted to driving on the right. Lucas make a beam converter which clips on and is yellow in colour in order to meet regulations in France (yellow lights are accepted in other continental countries). Alternatively, you can get this job done at the garage quite cheaply. Some countries regard the side-lights as parking lights only and demand that a motorist drives with dipped headlamps.

2 *Spares to take*

This is a matter of opinion and depends on where you intend to go. I drive a Ford, and when touring in Germany, Holland and France I work on the basis that Fords are just as common there as at home and that equally good service facilities are therefore available. On a trip to the Balkans, however, this may not be the case and it is advisable to take a few spares. Some manufacturers produce a holiday spares kit. This costs a few pounds, which is returnable, less a small fee and a charge for items used, when you get back from your holiday. These kits have been built up from the experience of the car firm and, as you have to limit the spares you carry, I think it is best to leave it up to them. If your manufacturer does not supply a spares kit, the R.A.C. provides one for most popular models. These are available to non-members.

Should you decide to build up your own spares kit, I suggest you include the following:

Light bulbs; contact breaker points or a complete distributor; fuses; condenser; plugs; coil; petrol pump; fan belt; inlet and exhaust valves and springs; cylinder head gaskets; top and bottom radiator hoses; tyre valves and caps; windscreen wiper blades; radiator and petrol filler caps; dynamo brushes; hydraulic brake spares and fluid.

There is no need to panic as you read this. I do not expect you to use these spares yourself – the main thing is to have them available if the need arises.

3 *G.B. plate*

You will require a G.B. plate for your car and, if you are towing, for your trailer or caravan as well (I am told the plate for the trailer is frequently overlooked). See that you get a plate of regulation size. Some countries are very sticky about this, and you may find entry refused should you arrive at the frontier without a plate or with an incorrect one.

4 *Odds and ends*

Conversion tables for petrol, showing the equivalent of gallons in litres, and for distance, turning kilometres into miles, are useful. These are supplied by the A.A., R.A.C. and several other bodies. Also available are diagrams of the continental road signs which you can stick on to your windscreen. These are not so important now that the United Kingdom uses similar signs, but you are certain to come across some which will be new to you. I always find that it is too late for my navigator to check the sign as we pass it, but it is nice to look it up to see what you have missed – in any case, it gives the driver an idea of what the policeman is stopping him for in advance!

Paperwork – the Documents Required

As I have said, the documents required to enable you to travel abroad have been reduced in number. Whereas a comparatively few years ago expert advice and assistance was regarded as essential when planning a continental holiday, today most people do all the paperwork by themselves. Let us have a look at the documents you will need to obtain one at a time.

Passport

These now last for ten years. An application form can be obtained from the Passport Office, the Ministry of Social Security Office (the old Labour Exchange), the motoring associations, banks and many travel agencies. A wife can be included on her husband's passport or she can – and I strongly advise this – have her own. Children can be included on either passport.

The "Green Card"

This is the international motor insurance card and is recognised nearly everywhere as showing that you have Third Party insurance, which is compulsory in most countries. Get this in plenty of time and see that it covers the whole period you will be abroad. Also ensure that it is marked, usually with a punch hole, for every country you will be visiting. Note that the Benelux countries insist that the card is marked for all three of them, even though you may only intend to visit one. The same applies to the four Scandinavian countries. It may, in fact, be worth getting your card to cover all countries. This will enable you to visit any country on the line of your route, or even to change your mind altogether – perhaps because of local weather conditions.

If you are taking a trailer or caravan with you, your card should be marked with a letter "F". It should also indicate the make of the 'van or trailer and show its chassis number.

If you borrow or hire a car, the card should show your name as the "user" as well as that of the owner.

One final point: Switzerland requires a duplicate Green Card which is retained in the event of an accident.

Triptych on Carnet de Passage et Douane

This form is no longer required for private cars, but if you tow a trailer for luggage or a boat or a trailer 'van the Triptych is essential. On entry, the Customs Officer takes the entry voucher and endorses the exit voucher counterfoil. If you have a trailer, do not drive straight through the Customs on leaving the country, even though it is often possible to do so, as the failure of the Customs Officer to detach the exit voucher could put you under suspicion of having sold the trailer there. These forms have to be obtained from the A.A. or R.A.C., but the latter club issues them to non-members.

International Driving Permit

Although British driving licences (not provisional ones) are accepted in most European countries, a few require an International Driving Permit. This is issued to any resident of the United Kingdom who is aged over eighteen and holds a full, valid British driving licence. The Permit is valid for a year and is issued by the motoring associations for a small fee.

International Camping Carnet

The Carnet is very useful in most countries and essential in Portugal, but it is still unnecessary in the United Kingdom. It can include both yourself and your family, and permits the holder to camp out at all sites organised by the national camping clubs. I do not say that you will not be allowed to use such sites if you are without a Carnet, but this is often the case. This is because the Carnet is evidence that the holder has Third Party insurance against claims arising out of accidents or damage to property whilst camping. The site owners quite rightly look upon this as very important. In addition, the holder of a Carnet often enjoys reduced terms, and the document is taken and held whilst you are at the site instead of your passport, which can be a great advantage.

Other Documents You Should Take
The only other documents which should be taken on your trip abroad are your car log book and your British driving licence.

Although I have not included them in the essential documents, please do not forget to take your travel tickets with you.

Planning Your Holiday in Europe

Unless you are proposing a short trip to Holland, Belgium or northern France which can easily be undertaken in a day, some planning is essential. Personally, I can see no merit in driving from dawn to dusk, or even longer, in order to reach some distant spot. A friend of mine travels colossal distances in a day, finishing completely exhausted and requiring a couple of days' rest to recover. He would do much better to take three days over his trip and enjoy it. Of course, the young man travelling alone or with a friend in a fast car can expect to travel much farther in a day than the man driving with his family.

Obviously, the first thing to decide is "where?" If there

is a place you really wish to visit, calculate whether it is within your maximum range, taking into account the length of your holiday, the number of hours you are prepared to drive each day and how much time, if any, is to be spent at places through which you will pass. When you estimate the distance you can cover in a day, remember that you will be on strange roads, and perhaps driving through hills and mountains – this will reduce your average speed. However, you are likely to encounter good roads on the whole – especially in countries on our side of the "Iron Curtain" – and less traffic, which will increase your average speed.

You must settle on your route and at the same time decide how you are going to cross the Channel. The route is very much a matter of personal choice. I always avoid "Autobahnen" like the plague and mark a route on my map which includes as many "green" roads as possible. I attempt to visit all places of interest not unreasonably out of my way and am always prepared, and in fact prefer, to stay a couple of nights at one or two places en route to my final destination. I find my dislike of motorways and similar main roads presents one or two problems. Most countries, in particular Germany, appear to have ceased signposting minor roads; all signs lead to the motorways. Enquiries made of local residents are equally unfruitful. They simply will not believe that you do not want to drive along their beautiful motorway. I have received such replies as "Surely you want the motorway" or "You should use the motorway, it is a fine road". Eventually, after I have explained that I want to see "their beautiful countryside", I usually obtain the required information. It is always when I am in doubt about the route that I have trouble with driving on the right. It is not that I am in danger, but rather that I automatically look to the left for road signs whereas, of course, they are on the right.

Having decided "where?", the next problem to be solved is "how?". This, of course, is a question of time and cost. The quickest way to get abroad is by air, but this is expensive – especially with a largish car. There is no doubt that to fly to Mittelkirke from Southend is ideal for the Londoner. The aircraft are comparatively small so that the number of passengers is limited. As a result, you can board just before take-off time and the wait for Customs at each end is very short. If you wish to fly, you can choose from the following routes:

1. Southend to Calais, Ostend or Rotterdam.
2. Lydd to Calais, Le Touquet or Ostend.
3. Hurn to Cherbourg.

All these routes are short and very popular. A year or so ago, it was thought that the short flights would be followed by an equally comprehensive series of long-haul routes taking motorists and their vehicles deep into Europe, but I believe there are only one or two operating.

The sea car ferry services are also very good. The hours of hanging about are gone, and driving on and off is a simple affair. In addition to numerous services to Ireland, you have an almost unlimited variety of routes to Europe to choose from:

1. Dover to Boulogne, Dunkirk, Ostend, Calais or Zeebrugge.
2. Newhaven to Dieppe.
3. Southampton to St Malo or Le Havre.
4. Harwich to Hook of Holland, Esbjerg or Kristiansand.
5. Tilbury to Esbjerg, Rotterdam or Göteborg.

6. Newcastle to Oslo, Bergen, Stavanger or Haugesund.
7. Hull to Rotterdam, Bremen or Hamburg.

The third alternative is to go by rail. British Railways have now joined the Continental Railways in running special car sleeper expresses. The centre in this country is Victoria Station in London. I will not pretend that this method is cheap – it is not. In fact, it is very expensive. How it compares with your normal means of travel depends on the type of holiday you favour. If, when you break your journey, you spend each night at an expensive hotel and stop for lunch at a first-class restaurant, the comparative costs will not be unfavourable; but if you take a packed lunch and pitch your tent at a camping site for a few pence a head, the additional cost of a rail sleeper is prohibitive. If the money is available, however, this is a very pleasant means of travel. You drive off the cross-Channel ferry onto a sort of bridge – a ramp which takes you into a position to drive straight onto the car-carrying rail transporter. The sleeping cars are next to the car carriers, so there is no distance to walk. You may save two or three days' travel each way and, of course, you add this to the length of your holiday at the chosen resort. In addition, you save many tiring hours of driving.

Sleeper expresses are railway travel at its best. They seem to collect the most helpful staff on these trains and the facilities are excellent. But I suppose it depends on how much you like driving as to whether or not this method of travel appeals to you. I love driving and, as we always stop to see anything of interest en route, our trips are leisurely and enjoyable. I myself would not consider any form of rail travel. If you do decide to use the sleeper expresses, be sure to book well in advance as they are usually pretty full.

Passing Through the Customs

I have passed through the Customs on many occasions. Although our own Customs have a reputation for being unnecessarily thorough and perhaps officious, I have never found them so. It is mainly a matter of honesty and organization. Do not say you have nothing to declare if you have bought items abroad, even should there be no duty to pay on them. Customs officers are expert at picking out people who are attempting to string them along. (Naturally, I am writing for the tourist and not for the enthusiastic amateur smuggler.) Have all the items you have purchased abroad together and declare them. In addition, have any necessary documents ready to hand. You want to get through the Customs rapidly and it is certain the Customs officers are just as keen to get you through quickly.

There is even less reason for any fuss at foreign frontiers. If your next holiday is your first trip abroad with a car, perhaps I can give you a few tips which might save you time. I do not say time and trouble because there is no need for trouble at Customs posts. When you are a few miles from the frontier make sure that you have all your documents ready and handy. You need your passport, your Green Card and, if the country you are about to enter requires it, your International Driving Permit.

As you approach the frontier, you will see a sign saying "Douane" or "Zoll" which indicates that you have just about arrived. At the Customs post you will most likely find lines of heavy transporters waiting to cross. Do not get behind these, as they will be waiting for a long time and you will find yourself stuck. Instead, drive on slowly until you reach the actual barrier or are stopped by a Customs officer. The heavy vehicles, and there may be dozens of continental trucks with trailers, are waiting to do their import and export paper-work and you do not want to get caught behind them (I always find these goods vehicles extremely interesting with their many wheels and huge driving cabs which are designed to take a relief crew). Should you arrive at a quiet post and not see a Customs officer, do not cross the frontier. As a rule, unless you are towing a caravan, they are not very interested in your leaving the country and you may well be waved through; but it is their privilege to make the decision, not yours.

You will find that the Customs officer or officers station themselves on the continental driver's side of the car. I find this convenient because it is simpler if my passenger handles the documents. Hand over the documents for all the occupants of the car. If there are two Customs men, one will check the passports and the other the Green Card. If you are towing, you may have to pull out of the queue to go into the office to have your Triptych stamped and the counterfoil detached. Some Customs officers, even though their country does not officially require a Triptych for a trailer, like to see one, so have it ready at all frontiers.

At reasonable hours at most frontiers you will find an office where you can exchange your money. Unless you have local currency or will not require it for some reason, it may pay you to change your money here as you will get the regulation rate of exchange, not that given by some shops and hotels which is highly profitable to themselves. If the Bureau is closed, do not worry because shops and garages accept the currency of neighbouring countries for a considerable distance inside the frontier. Incidentally, do not forget to check that you have all your documents before leaving a frontier. It is very inconvenient to have to go back for them, and you may not miss a passport until you want to change a traveller's cheque or leave the country at another frontier post.

Tips on Driving Abroad

I do not wish to insult my readers, but everybody has to drive on the "wrong" side of the road for the first time and most inexperienced drivers appreciate being able to benefit from other people's experience. I have already said that driving on the right is surprisingly easy. You do not need to worry about this.

The main problem is lack of visibility when overtaking. It is, of course, always bad driving to follow too closely on the tail of the car in front, but in Europe it is really dangerous. Hang well back before you start to overtake; in this way you will obtain maximum visibility. If you can rely on the experience of your front passenger, he or she can be of great value to you. I also advise the fitting of a wing mirror on the left-hand side – the off side when driving on the Continent.

It is ridiculous to give hand signals when driving on the right in a right-hand drive car and, in any case, Continentals make conscientious use of their flashing indicators. Whenever they intend to pull out, even if only slightly to pass a pedestrian, they will signal in plenty of time.

The double and single white (or yellow) lines are used a great deal, but they mean something on the Continent. It is an offence in some countries to cross an unbroken single white line, even if there is no other traffic about. The double lines work in the same way as ours; you may not cross them except when the line on your side is broken.

As we have now adopted the international road signs in

the United Kingdom, most drivers will be familiar with them – at least they should be. Danger signs are triangular. Briefly, triangular signs having the point upward show the hazard pictorially in the triangle; with the point downward, they indicate a major road ahead. Instruction signs are circular and show what is forbidden inside – an example is "No Entry". Signs providing information, such as "Parking", are square. Probably the traffic rule which provides the greatest danger for British tourists is that of "Priority to the Right". Unless there is a sign to the contrary, the roads coming in from the right, even the smallest, have priority and local drivers make full use of their rights. Where your road has priority over those joining it from the right, every intersection has a triangular sign with a vertical line crossed by a narrow line. The side road will have a stop sign on it. Watch this – it really is a menace to unwary visitors. Do remember to look for road signs on the right. This is difficult to get used to, especially when driving along a one-way road or a motorway.

Most continental police have the right – and use it – to fine traffic offenders on the spot; so either obey the local traffic laws or carry a good supply of ready cash with you.

Finally, remember that when a car flashes its headlights at you the driver means "Get out of the way – I'm coming through!" It is not the polite invitation for you to go first that it has become at home.

Accident Procedure Abroad

Most countries have regulations regarding accident procedure which you would be wise to look into before you leave. Some, including France and Spain, may ask you to leave a deposit to cover legal costs and fines. Others require you to carry a red reflecting triangle, which should be placed behind the car in the event of an accident or breakdown. In Spain, your car can be impounded if you have an accident, but bonds are available from the motoring organisations which may be left instead. It is an offence in some countries to move your car after an accident without police permission.

If you do have an accident abroad involving a Third Party, a report should at once be made to the insurance company that issued your Green Card. Always offer medical assistance; in some countries it is a legal requirement that you do so.

Cycle Camping in Europe

Whilst cycling on Britain's overcrowded roads is no pleasure – in fact, thoroughly dangerous – it is still a joy on the Continent (at least so I am informed, as I have now reached the stage of requiring comfort on holiday). On a correctly loaded bicycle you can pack about 75 lbs in panniers. There are no Customs or insurance documents to worry about; all that is required is your passport and Camping Carnet. British United Air Ferries carry cycles at a staggeringly low rate, whilst their passenger fares are also very reasonable. Over the Channel, most farmers will allow you to camp on their land – but do please ask first. You can always travel over too hilly or uninteresting country by train, or by bus if you have a folding cycle.

If you are still energetic, this is certainly a good way to have quite a cheap holiday abroad.

Chapter 17

Insurance: Be Sure – Insure

In the excitement and flurry of planning a holiday, insurance tends to get put off until later or is even completely overlooked. As a result, many people set off for the Continent with nothing more than the basic Third Party insurance provided by the Green Card or, if they are camping at home, merely with their car insurance. This is risky.

If you are a member of the Camping Club of Great Britain – as I hope you are or will be – you will have some basic insurance as one of the benefits of your membership. But you should at least consider all the various types of cover, even if you finally decide that the risk is not worth the premium. What type of insurance is available?

Insurance Cover Available

You can insure against almost anything. If you have an insurance broker you would do well to consult him, but the Camping Club of Great Britain, the Auto Camping Club and the Caravan Club amongst others will advise you and supply proposal forms. Although the premium for each risk is comparatively small, the total does mount up and you may therefore decide to balance the likelihood of any of the emergencies occurring against the cost and reduce your cover accordingly. Each camper must make his own decision, but remember that, whilst the possibility of your car running away on a camping site and wrecking somebody else's tent may be very remote, should it happen it could be expensive. Bear in mind also that in this country we rely on the National Health in times of illness – abroad, medical attention is expensive, and it can be very costly if someone falls ill or has an accident. You might even have to leave a member of your party in a hospital or a hotel, or perhaps remain abroad longer than you had expected yourself.

You can cover:

1. Baggage.
2. Accident and medical expenses.
3. Loss of cash, tickets or petrol coupons.
4. Camping equipment for fire, tempest, flood, theft and accidental damage.
5. Personal liability.
6. Cover off the road.
7. Breakdown or damage or loss of car.

If you intend to claim against loss by theft, you will have to notify the local police of the loss within a specified period, usually forty-eight hours. Regarding camping equipment, normal cover will be limited to include only loss through fire or theft whilst it is carried in your car. A special clause will have to be added to cover the risk of flood or tempest.

As far as baggage is concerned, you should specify any items of particular value, such as photographic equipment, musical instruments and tape recorders.

The personal liability policy should be considered. It covers the insurer and members of his family against their liability as private persons should they, through carelessness, cause injury to others or damage to other people's property. Careless use of a ball, stick or fire can result in a heavy claim. Cover for a large amount can be secured very cheaply.

Cover whilst the car is off the road is worth considering, as you may find that you are not covered by your policy when driving across a site. Most insurance companies extend their cover to the use of the car in these circumstances, but some do not and you should check up on this point. The owner of a site or field used for camping should absolve himself from any liability arising from accidents by displaying properly worded notices. This leaves it to the camper. There is a tendency to allow unqualified drivers to drive or move cars at camp sites, or even to receive driving lessons. This is extremely dangerous, especially when the vehicle is anywhere near tents or other campers.

It is a good idea to find out whether your car is actually covered during the crossing of the Channel by sea or air; if it is not, you may consider it worth your while to take out separate insurance.

Much of the insurance I have mentioned is included in R.A.C. and A.A. travel services, and is available from the Camping Club of Great Britain. These services are well worth considering.

Cover for Caravans

These notes only refer to 'vans which are used for touring; they do not apply to those which remain static at a site, for hire or for use as a residence.

Although the main dangers are, I suppose, accident damage whilst towing and fire, do not attempt to economise by covering certain risks only; it pays to go in for a "comprehensive" type of policy. Having made your decision, check it to see whether your cover is sufficiently high.

If there is any under-insurance, the insurers may have the right to reduce the amount they pay on your claim proportionately to the amount you are under-insured.

The main part of the policy covers only the 'van, not its contents. Personal effects such as luggage, watches and cameras have to be specified separately; failure to do so may considerably reduce any claim in respect of these items. In addition, some insurance companies insist that certain precautions be taken to minimize the chance of theft.

Should you let the 'van, whether to relatives or strangers, you are unlikely to meet any objection from the insurers, but you would be wise to notify them. You might, however, encounter an increase in premium here on the grounds that other people will not take the same care of your 'van as you do yourself.

Do not fall into the trap of thinking that you merely have to insure the 'van itself. Although a total loss would not exceed a few hundred pounds, a claim for damages made against you by a Third Party could run into many thousands. Remember that you or any member of your party could cause an accident by stepping out of a 'van carelessly, and that a 'van thoughtlessly parked could run into a tent, a car or another 'van. Ensure that you are covered for any accident caused by or through a vehicle which is towing a caravan. This risk has to be covered in the car policy and it is easily overlooked. In the legal view, the car or 'van is one unit when you are towing. Although many car policies contain no restrictions on towing a caravan, some do and it is a very sensible precaution to inform your insurer that you will be towing so that there can be no objection should you make a claim later. You should also make sure that your policy covers the 'van whilst it is not being towed, that is to say when it is being used as a home or standing still in the winter.

If you wish to tour outside the United Kingdom, make sure that your insurance company will extend its cover before you take out the basic policy. It is expensive to have to buy complete cover in order to make your holiday possible.

Insurance arrangements vary from time to time and from company to company, and it is a good idea to obtain expert advice before you apply for a policy. The camping and caravan clubs are happy to supply such advice to their members, and membership is well worth while for this point alone.

Chapter 18

Navigation, Maps and Map Reading

I always make a point of studying a map and discussing my
route with my family before leaving home. Despite ad-
vanced preparations, however, I usually find a navigator
necessary – in my case, as in most families, this is, of
course, my wife. Fortunately, she can read a map – unlike
the wife of a friend of mine who told me, when she was not
about, "She's all right when you are driving north: the
trouble comes when we go south as she wants to turn the
map upside down."

Nowadays, I do not bother to ask the R.A.C. or A.A.
for one of their excellent planned routes unless I am in a
hurry and require the quickest way. The advantage that
the R.A.C. and A.A. have when working out a route is a
knowledge of the latest road works, new roads and one-
way traffic. I find continental diversions very difficult to
follow. The Germans are my personal world champions at
signposting diversions. They are past-masters at leading
you into a field and leaving you there, taking you back
where you started, or deserting you when you have no idea
where you are. I remember once finishing up in the car
park of an army oil depot.

One method of route plotting is to list the places you
have to pass through showing all spots of possible interest
between them. This gives you a route plan very much like
those produced by the motoring associations. When I have
to pass through a large town, I always like to have a town

plan available. If you are going abroad, you can usually obtain these free from the National Tourist Centre of the country concerned prior to leaving. You can mark these plans beforehand so that you have a good idea which roads to take. It is all very well knowing that you have to find Karl Strasse somewhere on the left, but when the name is hidden by a tree, or a parked van, or is three storeys up, it may not be easy to find. If you know in advance that you want the third or fourth turning on the left, it is a great help. You may not know anything about local one-way systems, but it is a pretty good bet that every large square or circle shown on the map has a one-way flow. My experience of continental motoring is that most routes, particularly in towns, are signposted on the far side of the road for which you are searching and thus, when you see it, it is usually too late to make your turn. For this reason, advance planning on a map is a great help.

However and wherever you travel, you need a map, and the more you understand about it, the more it will help you enjoy your holiday. If you are a lightweight camper travelling on foot or on a bicycle, you should buy the one-inch-to-the-mile Ordnance Survey map. These show all the necessary detail, such as streams and foot-paths. Should the cyclist intend to cover a fair distance, he might find a half-inch-to-the-mile map better suited to his purpose. This covers twice as large an area for the same-sized map, but, naturally, omits some of the detail.

Most motorists use the maps in the R.A.C. or A.A. handbooks, an atlas of maps or those issued cheaply by the petrol companies. Most of these are four or five inches to the mile in scale and are sufficient as long as you keep to "A" or "B" class roads.

I have always found the maps provided by the oil

companies at a very small cost – abroad they are sometimes free – to be extremely good. Unfortunately, though,
in areas where there are few roads, such as the Yorkshire
Moors, the small roads are apt to peter out on the map and
you are faced with signs to unknown villages. This always
annoys me because surely it would not cost much more to
show the roads right through these large open areas. The
solution is to drive in a general direction by compass. Usually you get to a town or village you can recognise on the
map in roughly the right place.

Of course, the real answer to this is to get good maps,
but these are expensive and it seems extravagant to pay a
lot for maps of an area which you never expect to visit
again. In Britain the maps to buy, if you can afford them,
are those produced by the Ordnance Survey in one-inch
scale. Abroad, most, if not all, countries produce maps of
similar standard. If you are keeping to main roads on the
way to your destination, oil company maps are admirable,
but for local touring I always think it is a pity not to buy a
really good map which shows everything. You can miss a
great deal without one. Incidentally, the Camping Club of
Great Britain and Ireland gives map references of sites in
their lists based on the Ordnance Survey map. You can
find these from an ordinary map, but on Ordnance Survey
they are pinpointed exactly.

Once you have a map, you must know how to read it.
Most maps use similar and easily recognizable signs. For
example, on a one-inch map an arrow pointing downwards
indicates a gradient of more than 1 in 7, whilst a hill of
more than 1 in 5 is shown by two arrows. If you study the
key, you will have no difficulty in reading your map – in
fact, it will prove great fun.

Maps usually show the distances between towns. If

yours does not, you can either make a pretty accurate guess from the scale or you can use a map measurer. This device consists of a small wheel which you place on your map and run along the road. The distance is shown on a dial.

Chapter 19

Suggested Tours for Beginners

Before describing some suitable tours for beginners, I am going to make a few general comments which I feel may be helpful to those of you planning your first camping holiday.

Do not be too ambitious at first, especially if you have children with you. This applies both to the distance covered and to the number of stops you make. Driving too many miles can really kill enthusiasm. I know it is possible to cover great distances in a day on the Continent, but you must remember that motoring tends to be more tiring for the passengers than for the driver. Of course the driver has to concentrate, but the passengers become bored after a time – particularly on motorways – and can only sit and think just how uninterested they are. I am not opposing a long drive on the first day because here you have a journey which may be broken by a Channel crossing and, in any case, is supported by the initial excitement of actually setting off on holiday. But after the first day, driving should certainly not be overdone.

Another mistake which puts a damper on family enjoyment is the attempt to take in too many sites. Repeatedly erecting a tent for only one night will soon make everyone fed up with camping. I make it a point to stay at each site for at least three days, with the possible exception of the first and last nights; even then, I look for a site at a place worth a few days' stay.

The race to the sunny south of Europe has become an annual event for many families, but is it really worth it? This area is becoming more and more crowded each year (overcrowded would probably be a better word), and it is not uncommon for holidaymakers having finally arrived to find the glare of the sun far too much for them. It should also be remembered that when there is a storm in the sunny south it is usually a storm in a big way; moreover, that our own south coast is well up in the British sunshine league if not ahead. The weather just across the Channel is very similar, so if you visit northern France, Belgium or Holland you will stand a reasonable chance of good weather. All these countries have a great deal to offer the tourist and there are a countless number of camping sites. The roads may be cobbled in places, but this type of surface presents no difficulty if you take it at a reasonable speed. Generally, however, the roads are good.

Just as Wales, Scotland and Ireland all receive their fair share of rain and drizzle, so does the mountain country in Europe – although it is usually drier during the summer months. So, if you like mountainous scenery, it is well worth visiting Scotland, Wales or Ireland. At present, Eire is completely unspoilt; but the tourist industry is being encouraged and no doubt big hotels will soon spring up, together with the ice-cream and hot dog stalls. Spain is a typical example of what can happen within a few years. If you are undecided, why not try Eire before it goes commercial?

The following suggestions for camping tours are based on my own experience. None includes too many long days' motoring, and I have visited all the sites mentioned within the last year or two. Naturally I am writing for the person or family considering their first camping holiday in this country or abroad; I don't expect to convince veteran campers that my ideas are better than theirs.

Camping at Home

Unless you have some special reason to tour abroad, such as a particular sport or event, or someone to visit, or a determination to join in the race to the sun, I fail to see why anyone should holiday in Europe until they have explored their own country. What do you get abroad that you do not find at home? More consistent weather no doubt, but also in certain places excess heat, super storms at times, a higher accident rate on the roads, the cost and time in crossing the Channel – although it may be on a grander scale, the scenery in Europe is certainly no finer than that provided by Yorkshire, Wales, Scotland and the West Country.

As I live in London, I am naturally writing from the viewpoint of somebody starting from thereabouts. Everyone heading for Scotland from the Midlands will, I expect, make the trip without a break, whilst a reader living in the south will make at least one overnight stop on the way. Anyway, let us have a look at a few tours at home which I have made and enjoyed very much.

Yorkshire

We decided to break the journey halfway from London and, as we all dislike pitching the tent for only one or two nights, we looked for a site in an area which would interest us for a few days. We chose the Peak District, making Dovedale our target. This is a wonderful centre for walking and within a short distance of Matlock, Chatsworth House and Haddon Hall. Our choice of site was Back Top

Farm, Fenny Bentley, near Ashbourne, where two large fields have been allocated to camping. A small shop provides milk and food, and there are flush toilets and a wash room with running water. When I was there last, a hot water supply was being organised. The toilet accommodation is only small, but it was adequate even in August.

From Dovedale we drove on to Pickering, where there is a small site behind a café at Thornton le Dale which has a couple of small extension pitches, each taking two or three tents, about a quarter of a mile farther down the valley. The toilet facilities are at the café and there are none, or virtually none, at the extension sites. But you can shop at the café or in the pretty little town of Pickering. Within easy reach by car are the North Yorkshire Moors and several interesting towns, including York and Whitby. Whitby is a fine sailing resort, and has an attractive harbour and Abbey. York is a wonderful walled city with fascinating narrow cobbled streets and old-fashioned shops, and, of course, the famous Minster. There is an information centre in, I believe, Museum Street which provides plans of the city. As one would expect in the home of steam locomotives, there are two fine railway museums. One contains engines and rolling stock, and the other old tickets, time-tables and so on. Two more places which must be visited are York Castle Museum and the Old Debtors' Prison next door. In the former you will find the interiors of old cottages and an old street complete with shops, whilst there are authentic workshops, including a garage complete with vintage cars, in the latter. A walk round the city walls is also recommended. In case I have given the impression that the city is a museum-piece, let me assure you that there are many large, modern shops for the womenfolk.

Continuing north and driving through some beautiful country (the area around Sutton Bank, which is the home of the Yorkshire Gliding Club, is particularly lovely), we reached Lofthouse, which has several sites. We chose Studfold Farm, and this appeared to be best when we had a look at the others. You have to take a sharp left-hand turn after crossing a very narrow bridge to enter the camp. This is awkward for trailer caravans, but by no means impossible – in fact, I saw no one fail to make it, although there are many "scrape-marks" on the wall. As I left the site, I watched a delivery driver drive out towing a huge residential 'van behind a Land Rover and he made it first time. However, it is important to take the correct line if you want to get round without manoeuvring.

There is plenty to occupy your time here. You can go on walks across the Moors, or you can visit some of the abbeys and castles which the area abounds in. I found these disappointing on the whole, as most are completely ruined and require a great deal of imagination to visualise them in their original state. But Fountains Abbey and the neighbouring Fountains Hall, which was built from stones stolen from the Abbey ruins after the Dissolution, are really interesting. The area is also dotted with caverns, the nearest being Stump Cross Cavern, down which small parties are conducted by a guide. Lofthouse, incidentally, is a centre for the famous Yorkshire Dales.

On to the North Yorkshire Moors and miles from anywhere you will find the Rosedale Abbey camping site. Our first view of the site was a long stretch behind a protecting hedge running along a small river. This is rather dark and damp, but there is a second large camping area just down the road which is much better, being open and light, and is bounded on one side by the same river. The walks here are wonderful and again you are well within reach of the coastal towns.

Scotland

As is usual on our trips, we saw no reason to dash through the many beautiful places on our route when we visited Scotland, so we made a sort of circular tour. On the way north, we stopped for a few days at Bank Top Farm near Ashbourne, which I have already described.

From Ashbourne we drove north, crossing Hadrian's Wall, and on to the Forestry Commission site at Kielder (I understand that this camp is now run on behalf of the Forestry Commission by the Camping Club). The camp is adjacent to the North Tyne River, which provides fishing, and there are miles of forest for the walker. The camp lies in a very isolated spot and the approach is a long, almost deserted, road. The site is large and provided with a small shop, hot showers, and a hut for cooking and washing up. The trees provide protection from the wind, which blew a full gale whilst we were there.

From Kielder we drove to Edinburgh, where we pitched on the very large International site. This is a magnificent effort with large toilet facilities. We visited the camp during the Edinburgh Festival when it was naturally very crowded – overcrowded, in fact, as far as the facilities were concerned – but in more normal times it must provide most things that the average family camper could desire. Edinburgh requires little description from me; it is far too often written about – the magnificent Princes Street, its gardens, the Forth railway and road bridges, the Castle with its museum and war memorial, Holyrood Palace, the museums and shops. There are so many interesting places to visit that, even if it rains, a very happy holiday can be spent in Edinburgh. The country surrounding the city is also beautiful.

Our next stop was made at Aberdeen, the Granite City. We used the municipal site at Hazelhead Park. We saw the site at its worst – after a long period of heavy rain – but a friendly welcome from the warden made up for the saturated ground. The toilet facilities are very good and there is a caravan which is used as a shop, selling most of the usual items. The town itself is impressive, as well as providing the pleasures of the seaside. Do not miss an early morning visit to the fish market – until my visit I did not know that some types of fishes could be so large. The battle between the gulls and the merchants for the fish is also well worth seeing; I have never seen such enormous seagulls. Inland, there is beautiful scenery along Deeside, and it was through this that we drove to our next site.

From Aberdeen we turned inland along the River Dee and drove through the glorious mountain scenery of Ballater and Braemar, past Balmoral and down the Devil's Elbow with its famous hairpin bend. This, of course, is Scotland's famous winter sports centre. From here we continued into the heart of Perthshire, where we camped at Aberfeldy using the municipal site adjacent to the River Tay, which automatically makes it a fishing centre. The site is level with spotlessly clean toilets and washbasins. Aberfeldy is a small town of historical interest, particularly associated with General Wade and the Black Watch Regiment. It is in the middle of an area which provides just about everything for the camper, or any holidaymaker for that matter, except pleasures of the type associated with the Blackpool seafront. Surrounded by mountains and lochs, including Loch Tummel and Loch Tay, it is ideal for walkers, climbers and fishermen. On a hot day it is very tempting to swim from the quiet lochsides, but believe me the water is very cold indeed and I think it would be only too easy to get into difficulties. My advice is, either take great care or don't swim. Several interesting towns are within reach, including Perth and Stirling.

I looked at several sites in the area. Although one in particular was very scruffy, the others appeared to be first-class, so no trouble should be encountered when searching for a place to pitch. This is a wonderful centre for a holiday. You can drive and walk almost on your own, although you naturally find coach parties at the more famous beauty spots – especially at weekends. However, these parties soon disperse and they are very quiet compared with those met with at some of our seaside resorts.

Leaving Aberfeldy with great regret, we decided to make our return journey to London through the Lake District. Although I had read in the camping magazines that motorised campers are not really wanted and only lightweight campers encouraged, we found a very pleasant farm site at Limefitt Farm, Troutbeck. The facilities offered were an "electrical" wash room, flush toilet accommodation and a shop in the farmhouse. The site is bounded by a river and approached by a steep grassy bank, which wants watching if you arrive in a car in the dark. I read in the Camping Club List that this site has been enlarged to include a licensed club, but I hesitate to call this an improvement – it is all a matter of opinion. The area provides all the attractions of the Lake District and is ideal for walkers and drivers. Even motorists will find that they will have to leave their cars and walk. Personally, I found the Lake District very similar to Scotland, but on a smaller scale and I rather wished I had visited the Lakes first. However, I am probably being unkind and unfair, and I thoroughly recommend the Lake District to campers.

Our route is easy to plot on a map, but to those who dislike pitching and breaking camp I can say that most of the places I visited provide sufficient attractions for a holiday at one site alone. Certainly lightweight campers would find sufficient walking and climbing at the Lake District or Aberfeldy without wanting to move on. This also applies to the camping sites described in Yorkshire.

Camping in Europe

I have already repeated several times in this book my advice not to drive too far afield on your first tour and I now do so again. Nothing is so certain to ruin a holiday as erecting a tent on a dark, wet evening when you have already exhausted yourself and your family by driving three or four hundred miles. Take it easy at first, and enjoy both your driving and your camping.

How far you go must depends on the time and money available. A schoolmaster I know vanishes in the summer with his family, car, trailer and tent for six weeks at a time, but for the purposes of this chapter I am going to assume that the reader has only one or two weeks to spare. With reasonable driving, this can suffice for a trip to northern Europe or Ireland.

Holland, Belgium and Luxembourg

Holland is a wonderful country for your first camping holiday. It is hard to imagine a more friendly people – to the British anyway – and the countryside, although flat, is of great interest with its canals and windmills, whilst many of the towns are filled with historically exciting buildings and museums. The shopping centres are not neglected and most towns are well supplied with first-class shops to keep the womenfolk amused. Much the same applies to Belgium. The Belgians are by no means so fanatically pro-British, but they are friendly and the country is well worth a tour. Both countries are small and thus it is possible to visit most places from one, or at the most two, central sites, provided that you have a car available. As they are neighbours, both can be explored during one holiday and the fact that they are flat, especially Holland, can be a great relief for the caravan or trailer tent owner who fears for his car or his driving ability on his first trip abroad.

There are several possible routes to Belgium and Holland, but the most popular are by air ferry to Middlekirke or by ship to Ostend – both deposit you close to the end (or beginning, whichever it is) of the Brussels motorway. Belgian sites vary greatly, ranging from the disgusting to the first-class. Close to the sea and airport is Bruges, where you will find the St Michael site. This is an excellent site, being quiet (although near the main road), clean and well kept, and provided with hot showers and restaurant. It is guarded at night by the owner and his dog. The pitches are marked off and the grass is kept short, but as the ground is level it does not really matter which pitch you are allotted; in any case, I am sure it would be changed without question on request.

Bruges is a wonderful city; you can climb up to the belfry of the famous tower – don't attempt this, though, unless you are happy about heights. Even going up the narrow, winding staircase can be frightening, especially as you can see down – a long way down – through cracks in the floor. I strongly advise against taking children up if there is any doubt about their head for heights. From the top, the view is fabulous. The town square, the museums with their old lace and the bridges should all be visited. Built up to five hundred years ago to take an occasional carriage, the bridges carry an unending stream of motor coaches without complaint or collapse, which is a great tribute to their designers and builders. Whilst at Bruges do not miss a night trip by boat around the canals – it is a must! Also visit Zeebrugge with its mole and museum. There is a sea coast with miles of sand and dunes.

Brussels is worth a visit. With its shops – the main shopping street is heated – buildings, and the usual theatres, cinemas and night clubs, it has all the facilities expected of a capital city. I have not camped there, but it can easily be reached from Bruges. If you wish to do no more than cross the city, you can do so by using the motorway which passes through the centre.

From Bruges or Brussels it is an easy drive to Anseremme, another interesting town where the rivers Meuse and Lesse meet. A neighbouring town at the foot of the Ardennes is Dinant. From here you can take a river trip or walk or climb, or better still do all three. There are several sites in this area, although I have yet to find one that reached the standard I like. But the area is such that it is worth putting up with a lower standard or finding, as we once did, a friendly landowner who will allow you to pitch on his land. Not so far away, however, are the famous Grottos of Han where, as well as visiting the Grottos themselves, you will find a site to which I have been recommended but have never visited. To get there from Dinant you have to drive through the wonderful mountainous country of the Ardennes. This area is really hilly and can be a great strain on a car, especially if carrying or pulling an unreasonable weight.

From here we visited Luxembourg – a land of hills and vineyards. We camped at the town of Luxembourg itself, using the Itzigerste site. It was small but good, lying in the valley on the bank of the river Alzette.

Turning towards home, we pitched on the municipal site at Rotterdam – another really good site with showers, restaurant and shop. Rotterdam had to be completely re-built after the War and today is a new city. The shopping area is therefore very modern and is free of vehicles. Rotterdam is within easy reach of Amsterdam. At the former city, you can take a boat trip round the docks and at the latter a boat trip around the canals. Neither should be missed. If you like the seaside, try Zandvoort; it is complete with all the usual tourist amenities and restaurants.

Whilst in Holland I recommend a visit to Oosterbeck, where you will find the Arnhem cemetery and museum, as this is where the paradrop actually took place. A very short run away are the famous bridges. I used the De Bilderberg site, where the grass is like a bowling green and the other facilities equally good. Whilst I did not inspect them, I noticed several other good-looking sites in the area.

The famous Friday morning cheese market at Alkmaar is interesting. Cheeses arrive by barge which are unladen by staff in traditional dress. Even if you are not interested in cheese, the market provides a very good photographic souvenir.

Germany

Many parts of Germany are well worth visiting, amongst them being the North German Plain and the Black Forest. My trip takes you to Cologne and Aachen. If you live in the southern part of England, it is not too difficult to reach Cologne in one day, but it is a long drive and the distance is just about the limit I would advise. You can spend a night at an English coast site (although I have never done this) or stop at Bruges at the St Michael site which I have already described; this is on your direct route, providing you use Ostend. Alternatively, you could drive up to Holland for a day or two.

There are several sites near Cologne, including some actually on the bank of the Rhine. We use the Familiehzelt Platz (Camping Platz) der Stadt Koln, which lies at the foot of the Autobahn bridge on the other side of the river from the cathedral. This is a well-equipped site, although the authorities tend to allow it to get too crowded at times of peak popularity. The reception we received could not have been more friendly. The city is, of course, famous for its cathedral, but the shops and beer cellars, a river trip and the surrounding countryside are absorbing enough to keep you happy for the whole of your holiday. If you wish to visit the town from the site, I recommend using the tramway. You are likely to have difficulty parking your car if you try to take it into the city centre.

If you have a car, do not miss the chance of driving along the Ahr Valley whilst you are in the vicinity. This is a wine-growing area, and along the Valley you will find delightful little towns, all attempting to sell you their local vintage. Of these, the old-world town of Münstereifel is worth a visit by itself.

If you have time when you leave Cologne, drive down to the old Roman town of Aachen. The Roman remains, the old but not so ancient German buildings and the market will keep you amused. The site, quite a good one, is by the river, and again I would advise you to leave your car there and travel into the town on foot or by public transport.

The Autobahnen provide first-class high speed travel, but if you wish to see Germany plot your route from maps and use the old roads. Even cheap maps are marked to show local beauty spots, places of interest and the more scenic roads.

Chapter 20

Amusement and Entertainment

Whilst I like quiet holidays and therefore avoid busy resorts by as many miles as is convenient, I do like to spend
the day in a reasonably energetic manner. There are many
ways of doing this: you can walk, climb, canoe, sail, fish
or swim, providing the weather is kind to you. If you have
your own boat or canoe, you can trail it, putting most of
your camping and personal gear on the trailer; in this way
you will leave your car uncluttered. If you are unlucky
with your weather, then the time may be better spent in a
more cultural fashion, visiting museums and so forth. It is
surprising how many extremely interesting local or specialist museums there are if you look for them – those at
York which I have already mentioned are typical examples.

It is very important not to overdo things whilst on holiday. It can be extremely dangerous to spend fifty weeks
sitting at an office desk and in front of a television set, and
then to attempt ambitious climbs or expeditions during
your couple of weeks' holiday. Plan your trips within your
ability, taking into account both your physical condition
and your technical skill. You cannot just buy or hire a
sailing dinghy or canoe and expect straightway to put to
sea or canoe along fast-flowing rivers. This can only result
in disaster. The Central Council of Physical Recreation
run weekend courses covering most outdoor and athletic
activities; it would be well worth your while to go on one
of these, or to send one of your family. One "expert" in the

family will prevent an accident resulting from complete ignorance, such as standing up to change places in a boat.

Before you rush off on holiday with your boat, swimming or fishing gear, make sure that you have the appropriate licence; most fishermen require one and, similarly, the majority of river authorities charge a small sum for using their banks and locks. To avoid wasting your first weekend you should obtain all the necessary licences before you start off. Even if you are a bit of an expert, always seek and take note of local advice. This particularly applies to those who boat. The local fishermen or harbour-master will often be able to warn you of windy weather ahead on what appears to the visitor to be a beautiful and settled day.

Photography

The majority of campers take photographs, and all most of us require is a fairly cheap camera. With a small, light 35-mm camera, which can be carried by the most "lightweight" camper, you can produce a series of first-class colour transparencies, for use with a projector and screen, or colour photographs.

Walking

Walking, of course, brings us back to lightweight camping. If you walk in a group, it is important to ensure in advance that all the members of the party can keep up. It will spoil the holiday for both the fast walkers who have to hang back and the slower ones who cannot keep up if the party is too mixed. You should certainly not be too ambitious at first; remember that three miles an hour is a pretty good average on level ground, and that rough country will slow you down considerably. Watch, too, the weight of your pack; 30 lbs does not sound much, but it is not a weight which can be handled easily – practice and training are required. You must break yourself in easily. Start with an hour's stroll and gradually work up to a full day's walk.

Most campers only walk from car to tent and from a near-by car park to the various beauty spots shown in the local guide books; these people miss a lot. Walking over open country has so many attractions that I am always amazed how few campers try it. Of course you can travel to a central site by car, but try walking from there. Camping and walking are a great combination. The wind and fresh air and sun provide a wonderful feeling of well-being, and you soon become really interested in the local fauna and flora.

You do not need much equipment for walking, nor is it expensive. Boots or some other type of substantial footwear are the first requirement. Good walking boots only cost a few pounds and last for years. Buy a sufficiently large size to enable you to wear thick woollen socks with them. As exposure is a thing to be avoided, I consider a roomy, windproof and showerproof anorak to be essential. Of the two, it is more important that your garment be windproof than showerproof as you can always carry a plastic raincoat or cape (it is probably advisable to do so if you do your walking in this country). The anorak should be buttonless, hooded and of the type that pulls over the head. Preferably, it should be of close-woven material and have elastic cuffs, whilst a crutch strap to hold it down and big pockets are also desirable. Finally, you will need a rucksack for spare socks and a water bottle (if it is not carried separately), maps and a compass.

If you are travelling alone or in a small party, I cannot emphasise too much the importance of map and compass. A petrol company map, or an A.A. or R.A.C. handbook is just not sufficient. You must get a good Ordnance Survey map of at least an inch-to-the-mile scale. They cost a little more, but are not really expensive. For a compass I recommend the Silva type. It is sold by most camping suppliers and is very easy to use (in any case, it comes complete with a little book of instructions). I also advise you to take some emergency rations.

I am told that an altitude of 5000 ft in Great Britain is the equivalent of 8000 ft in the Alps as far as temperature and wind are concerned. So, if you are doing anything more ambitious than walking round the edge of the moors or wild country, good equipment is essential.

If you like to do your walking in organised parties, both the lightweight section of the Camping Club of Great Britain and Ireland and the Auto Camping Club arrange trips, varying from simple rambles to ambitious expeditions.

Swimming

Swimming is a natural activity of the camper, whether he travels by car, on two wheels or on foot. At some stage he is sure to arrive hot and sticky at a beautiful lake or river, which makes the thought of a swim irresistible. Giving way to this temptation, however, can be dangerous, for your hot body will be plunged into cold – often icy-cold – water. It is unwise to swim far and for too long; you can easily become cold and weak without noticing it, and may find yourself a fair distance from the bank and unable to reach it. We have all heard, and often ignored, the advice to leave a reasonable period of time after a meal before you swim. But it is good advice and you neglect it at your peril. A camper tends to visit isolated places, so if you get into difficulties help may not be as readily available as at a crowded seaside resort. Do not fool about, therefore, or get out of sight of immediate help.

Underwater Swimming and Skin Diving

These sports are both exciting and enjoyable, and fit in well with a camping holiday. In Britain, the best sea waters for diving are found off the coasts of Scotland, Wales and the West Country; the Cornish coast is particularly popular. Lakes and rivers are suitable for underwater swimming, but to give good visibility the water must obviously be clean and free of weed (the latter can also trap the unwary or careless swimmer). All suitable underwater swimming waters have several camp sites in the area, so you will have no trouble finding a base.

Fig. 88

To take up underwater swimming you require fins (see Fig. 88), a face mask (see Fig. 89) and a snorkel tube (see Fig. 90). The mask should fit well so that it does not leak and have an unbreakable window. Snorkels vary in length from 12 ins to 18 ins and are strapped to face masks. The mouthpiece of the snorkel is held by biting on two rubber lugs at each side of the air aperture. At first, avoid some of the tubes with complicated valves and get a simple one with a crook at the bottom. Fins must also fit well.

In British waters it is too cold to stay in long without some form of body protection and you can obtain both "wet" and "dry" suits. Wet suits allow a little water to enter which covers the body and warms up to form an insulation which is held into the suit in the form of air bubbles. This type of suit leaves only the feet and hands

Fig. 89

uncovered. Dry suits are made of thin rubber or plastic, and as a rule old woollen clothing is worn underneath. Suits should be rinsed in clean water after use in the sea; they should be stored out of direct sunlight.

It is very easy to get too far from your base or from help when skin diving and it is very unwise to swim alone if you are inexperienced, so I strongly advise anyone interested to take a course at a school approved by the national association, the British Sub Aqua Club. The Central Council of Physical Recreation and the Youth Hostels Association arrange organised swimming and diving holidays which are suitable for the novice.

Fig. 90

A final word of advice: never let children go underwater swimming or skin diving alone.

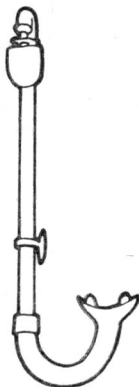

Fishing

Whereas river fishing can be expensive, sea fishing is cheap – free if you use a boat for which you do not have to pay a hire fee. The danger with fishing is that it can become a time-consuming drug, and unless your wife (or husband) also catches the disease you are heading for matrimonial trouble if you get it.

Fishing is great fun, all the way from the efforts of a child with a net or a cane, string and a worm to the very expensive, comprehensive outfit used by the dedicated angler. Fishing fits in well with lazy camping holidays. Given fine weather, the angler can look forward to long, restful days interrupted only with moments of excitement as a bite is obtained.

Sailing

Boats, or rather sailing dinghies, are expensive to buy new. If you purchase a secondhand dinghy, either deal with a reputable dealer or obtain the services of a knowledgeable friend. Ownership will be unreasonably expensive if you only intend to use your boat for a few days of the year and you will be well advised to hire locally. You are also faced with deciding which kind of boat to buy or hire. I will deal with canoes separately, and motor cruisers are outside the scope of a camping book, but sailing boats or dinghies which can be trailed or carried on the car roof are of definite interest to the camper.

Inflatable Boats

You can buy or hire tough rubber dinghies which can be sailed or propelled by an outboard motor. These are very safe and manoeuvrable, some nine or ten feet long, and can carry three or four people (see Fig. 91). Even should you get amongst some rocks and tear the fabric, do not panic because the boat is divided into several separate sections and, although filled with water, will remain afloat. Avoid dragging the dinghy across stones, rocks or sand as this can damage it. Such treatment is, in fact, unnecessary as two

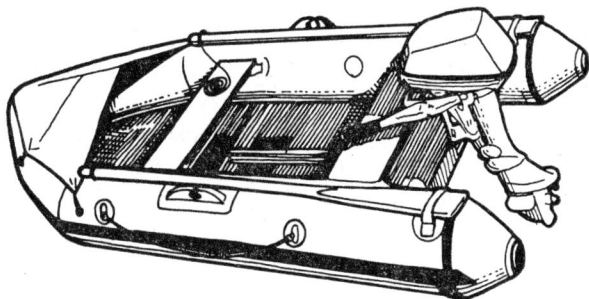

Fig. 91

boys can carry the boat without difficulty. Take great care that you moor your boat securely. It stands high out of the water and is very light, so it is easily caught by the wind.

These rubber dinghies pack into a small space and are easy to inflate. If there is a disadvantage, it is the length of time it takes to deflate them. Allow yourself plenty of time for this.

The Sailing Dinghy

Like fishing, sailing is a disease which it is easy to catch. If you have no decided opinion on the type of dinghy you require, make enquiries of your local sailing club. As a rule, clubs only accept members who sail the type of boat approved by the club and used by the club members. Some types, such as the famous G.P. 14, are very popular and accepted almost everywhere, but others are confined to small areas and you may be faced with selling your boat

and buying another before you can join a club. The G.P.
14 is 14 ft long, with a crew of two for racing purposes. It
will carry four in comfort and safety when just cruising.
Some boats also take an outboard motor.

You can obtain sailing boats of the "pram" type quite
cheaply and they cost even less in kit form. These are
quite suitable for fishing or pottering, but no self-respect-
ing sailing club member would be seen dead in one. However, if you do not intend to become a club member they
are great fun.

In addition to the boat you will require a trailer or, if
your boat can be carried on the roof, a suitable roof rack

Fig. 92

(see Fig. 92). You also require a launching trailer to transport the boat from your parking place to the water. Some
boats can themselves be used as roof racks (see Fig. 93),
but these fit into no recognised class. Another essential
accessory is a life jacket for each member of the family.
Make sure you get a good one of a foolproof design. You

are sure to go in at some stage and, whilst this is no
danger to a properly equipped sailor, it can mean death to
a person who is without a life jacket or wearing one which

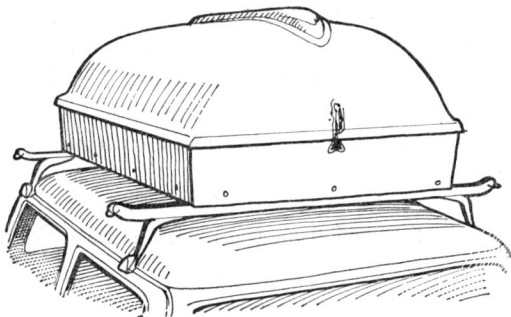

Fig. 93

is badly designed. Once you decide to buy a boat it is worth
noting that very often the price quoted does not include
sails, and you must take the cost of these into account
when working out whether you can afford to purchase.

To launch the boat into a river, push the boat on its
launching trailer backwards into the water – with the sails
already rigged if the wind is blowing off shore. Whilst one
member of the crew removes the trailer and pushes it
safely ashore, the other holds the painter to secure the
boat. Should the wind be blowing on shore, you will have
to launch the boat with the sails unrigged and rig them
whilst on the water.

If you are launching into the sea, you are almost certain
to meet some surf and breakers. Push the boat, with the
sails rigged, on its launching trolley as close to the water as
possible. If there is shingle between smooth ground and
the sea, push the dinghy over the stones on rollers. You

can get roller bags from a dealer. Whilst one person secures the boat with the painter, the other pushes the trolley and the rollers safely above the high-water marks. They then wait for a small wave and push the boat out as the wave recedes. The helmsman and crewman jump in and sail clear of the surf.

You must not overlook the unfortunate fact that you cannot approach a stretch of water, or even the sea, and launch where and when you like. If you wish to sail on rivers, you usually have to pay a small sum for a licence from the local conservancy board and, of course, fees have to be paid for every lock that you pass through. Many lakes and most smaller stretches of water are reservoirs and owned by a water board who let sailing rights to clubs. Launching ramps into the sea are owned by fishermen, yacht clubs or the local council. In the case of the council, you will probably be able to obtain the right to launch for a nominal amount. Yacht clubs may accept you as a temporary member, whilst the fishermen will no doubt allow you to use their ramps, provided that you have the courtesy to ask first.

Canoeing

Don't make the mistake of looking on canoeing as child's play. To quote the magazine *Small Boat* it is "a sport in the fullest sense and an elating sport at that. It offers fun galore, pleasure, excitement and adventure unlimited, but competition-wise it demands the highest degree of physical fitness, immense stamina and technical skill." Canoeing can be enjoyed by the old and young alike. You can pitch your frame tent near suitable water and tour in your canoe, returning to the site each evening or even each meal time. A lightweight camper can fit all his gear into a canoe and use it as his means of transport. You can potter about on lakes, rivers and canals miles away from busy towns – or even actually in busy towns, but away from the noise and traffic. If boating appeals to you, canoes certainly provide the cheapest way of starting on the water.

The best way to take up canoeing is to join a club; they usually have canoes available to members who wish to get the hang of things without the expense of purchasing. The Central Council of Physical Recreation runs canoeing courses, as do many local councils and youth organisations. It is advisable to learn how to handle a canoe before you or your children set off on the water in one as you will almost certainly overturn at some stage. With experience it is easy to right an upturned canoe or bale out of it, so do not let it worry you. But it is unwise to canoe alone if you are inexperienced and you should never let inexperienced children go out unsupervised.

Nowadays in this country, a "canoe" is popularly regarded as a fully-decked craft in which the occupant or occupants face forward and use a double-bladed paddle to propel the craft. This is really a kayak. The open, Red Indian type is seldom seen in Britain. Fig. 94 shows a single-seater and Fig. 95 a two-seater. If you put a spray cover over your cockpit and wear a waterproof jacket or anorak (see Fig. 96), you will be able to face anything our climate offers.

Most canoes used are home-made rigid craft – usually a wooden frame covered with canvas on the same lines as the old wooden aircraft. These are very strong, although they do not appear to be so. Other types have a plywood or fibre glass skin. You can also get a folding type which packs into a canvas bag when dismantled.

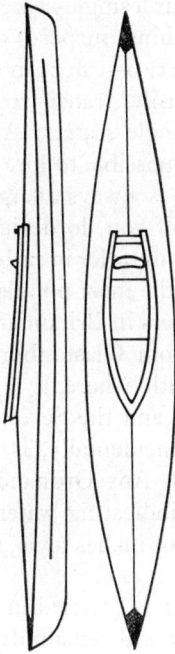

Fig. 94

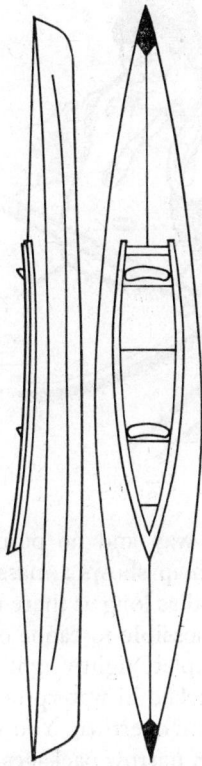

Fig. 95

You can build a canoe at home with only a basic skill and tools. The cost of a kit is only half that of the finished article. Most canoes are either single-seaters or built for two. Enthusiasts nearly always favour a single-seater, but for teaching purposes or a family, one two-seater canoe is more easily transported than two single-seaters. Although it is possible to hire a canoe, there is always a large demand, so if you do decide to hire get your order in early.

Fig. 96

Probably the most popular canoeing rivers in Britain are the Wye, from Glastonbury to Monmouth where it becomes tidal, and the Severn. The Wye, incidentally, is a right of way and no permit is required. Any Ordnance Survey map shows a mass of blue lines indicating waterways, and as long as there is a depth of four inches or so, it will be possible to canoe on any of them.

A complete lightweight camping kit can be carried in a canoe packed in waterproof containers. It will remain dry even if you overturn. You will have to break your kit down into long, narrow packages in order to fit it into the narrow bows and stern of the canoe. Cooking gear, tinned food, fuel and water containers can be packed loose, but make sure that you will not lose anything should you capsize. Always pack your gear out of the way; never have it in the cockpit (see Fig. 97).

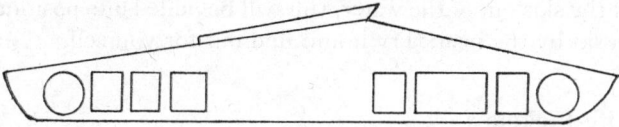

Fig. 97

Just as when you plan a walking tour, do not expect to travel too far in your canoe at first. Hands blister just as easily as feet. You might reasonably expect to cover fifteen miles in a day on still water. Do not forget to allow time for locks.

If you wish to know more about canoes and canoeing you might read:

1. *Canoeing* by P. W. Blandford (Foyles)
2. *Canoes and Canoeing* by P. W. Blandford (Lutterworth Press)
3. *Know the Game – Boating* (Educational Productions)

Water Skiing

This sounds a very expensive and difficult sport, but it need not be the case. You can purchase or hire a large variety of inflatable boats, all of which will take an engine of some 20 hp which is sufficient power to make water skiing possible.

Although I am aware that the "experts" dispute this strongly, I think you will be surprised how easy it is to water ski – perhaps not with the style of an "expert", but certainly well enough to give you lots of fun. Usually beginners take off from a platform or a low bank, but if you take up a position in waist-deep water and float on your back with your feet together, knees well bent and the front of the skis out of the water, you will be pulled into position to ski by the boat. Try it and find out for yourself.

Life Jackets

To avoid repetition I have hardly mentioned the one item that is essential to all forms of water sport – that is the life jacket. The British Standards Institute, the Consumers' Association and the boating press are constantly warning about ineffective life jackets. I suggest you take expert advice before buying, but do buy. All the experts wear them and it is even more important that the novice should do so.

The British Standards Institute has stated: "Products are often loosely referred to as life jackets, buoyancy aids, floating jackets and buoyant smocks. High pressure advertising and misleading labels mean that retailers and purchasers alike are frequently unaware that these are not really life jackets at all. A person wearing such an aid who falls into the water and becomes exhausted will soon drown. Bodies have been found face downwards in the sea wearing 'jackets' that failed to keep them alive when they could not longer swim."

Properly approved life jackets, costing only about £1·75 more, will not only keep you afloat but will actually turn you over so that your face is kept clear of the water – even when you are exhausted or unconscious.

The British Standards calls for a minimum of 30 lbs buoyancy, but this buoyancy must be correctly distributed. The jacket must also turn the wearer face upwards in five seconds from entering the water and hold him inclined backwards to face the oncoming waves.

Many types of jackets now have British Standards

approval, and some of them are easy and convenient to wear, not getting in the way of your arms as you paddle a canoe. The British Standards kite mark is a first-class safeguard. Look for it when you choose life jackets for yourself and your family.

Final Remarks

I suppose any form of activity which takes place in the country or in the sea links up happily with camping. You could equally well become a Go Kart enthusiast, as many of the tracks are situated on the coast or in parts of the country in which camping is well worth while.

My family and I camp primarily because we like the fresh air and freedom, and we fill in our time with leisure activities. If you become involved in any of the activities I have mentioned, you can easily find yourself becoming dedicated to one particular sport and then camping becomes nothing more than cheap accommodation whilst you participate. When this happens, the family part of the holiday may well come to an end and this is a great pity. If you take my advice, you will keep to camping for a quiet restful holiday and take care that any other activity in which you participate remains nothing more than a light-hearted recreation.

Part Five

On the Site

Chapter 21

The Camping Site

Campers differ in their requirements of a site, from those who want nothing more than the corner of a field to those who demand solidly-built toilet blocks, hot showers, shops, a room for washing clothes, a rest room or lounge with a television set and a children's playroom. Personally, I think the ideal site is somewhere between the two. I consider good, clean toilets to be essential, and I like a hot water supply, as this saves my personal gas supply, and showers; a shop selling gas, milk and food is also very useful. The remainder surely do not form part of camping life. However, I do think a play area is important. Children like to play football and cricket (and so do I), and it is very useful to have an area set aside for this purpose – it is annoying to find your car or tent being hit by balls and this can result in expensive repairs.

A great deal of information regarding sites and their facilities can be obtained from the list issued to members by the Camping Club of Great Britain and Ireland, and from other lists which are on the market. All the camping magazines run a regular page of readers' comments on sites visited, but it must be remembered that these only describe the sites at a particular time. A site which merits and receives a glowing description in June or late September may be grossly overcrowded in August. The best method of obtaining information about sites is the personal recommendation of friends whom you know have similar tastes to yourself; it is surprising how many of your friends will turn out to be enthusiastic campers when you begin to discuss holidays with them.

What sort of holiday do you want? If you are camping for the sake of open air and the freedom to go where you like when you like, a well-conducted site consisting of a reasonably level field with mown grass and satisfactory waste disposal, together with clean toilets and a water supply, is sufficient – at least this satisfies me. You may well be prepared to carry a supply of water and to make your own toilet arrangements, in which case you will want no more than the field. On the other hand, if you are a hotel-minded person and only camping to save expense, you will, I am sure, require the full treatment. You will demand a site which has first-class toilet arrangements, hot showers, a washroom with drying facilities and poss- ibly even a television lounge (believe it or not, such sites can be found). If this should be your type of camping and you discover a suitable site, you would be wise to book in advance. This is usually possible, but it will be worth confirming that the proprietor actually reserves a pitch for you and, even better, can inform you of its situation and size when you book. Some site owners are inclined to accept a booking fee but take no action, hoping to squeeze the campers who arrive into the space available. It has been known for holidaymakers who have booked their pitches to arrive to find the site overcrowded or even com- pletely full. Here again, recommendations from friends are of great value and, of course, try to avoid peak periods. Luxury sites are not common, and if you like this sort of thing you will no doubt settle in and remain there for the whole of your holiday. For this reason I repeat, book a pitch in plenty of time.

If, like me, you prefer to tour and not to book your site in advance, you will be well advised to plan your route and then decide upon the areas in which you propose to camp. Now have a look at the local sites in the Camping Club List and any other list that you have available. These lists show the facilities available at each site. The Camping Club sites are pretty basic as a rule, but they are very clean and well run. Next read through the readers' comments on sites in the camping magazines; these are first-hand accounts of sites used recently and usually say at what period of the year the site was visited. This, as I have said already, is important. Early in the year a site will be clean and lushly tufted with grass, whereas at the end of the season, with the best intention in the world, the facilities will be somewhat battered, and the grass worn and brown; you must make allowances for this. If you are intending to camp abroad, a book entitled *Europa Camping and Caravanning* provides much useful information on sites on the Continent. You should be able to obtain a copy of this from your public library.

Arriving at the Site

Having chosen your site, the next thing is to find it. As the signposting in this country is poor in the best of cases and often non-existent, it will pay you to make a route card for the last few miles. Many sites are in out-of-the-way spots and hard to find, especially if you arrive in bad weather conditions or in the dark. I advise early arrival, allowing sufficient time to pitch and settle down in daylight, and to move on to the next site if you do not like what you see. Despite any recommendations you may have received, it pays to walk round the site before signing in. We always have a look on arrival and, if we like the general layout and amenities, then look for a suitable pitch. Out of common courtesy, ask the site owner or manager for permission to look round before you do so. It is hardly ever refused, but if it is I would advise you to drive on. You have every right to be suspicious of a site run by someone who is obviously unfriendly.

What are you looking for when inspecting the site before booking in? I think the toilet block comes first, but there are other very important items – waste collection, for example, is vital. If the camp organiser allows old food tins and wrappers to be chucked into open pits or bins and fails to maintain a regular collection, you will find his site swarming with flies and wasps. Is the water tap just a tap nailed to a tree or post? If so, you may find that the ground around it is nothing more than a bog. If the site is isolated, does it have a shop and, if so, can you get what you consider to be necessities? Is the toilet accommodation sufficient for the number of campers present, bearing in mind the morning rush? If you demand a site with showers, what are these like? Look for any items you regard as essential – is the site too crowded? If you light your tent from your car battery, can you park your car close to the tent and, if so, can you do this without the danger of getting bogged down? If you have children, is there space for them to play? Finally, are the fees reasonable for the facilities offered? Incidentally, don't forget that the fees may have been increased since the information was provided for your list.

Camping sites tend to bunch together. This is due mainly to the natural demand for them in beauty spots and possibly to certain councils being sympathetic towards organised camping. In view of the poor signposting, it is worth making sure that you have found the site that you intended to use. It is too late, when you have paid and settled in, to move to the site you originally chose which may have much better facilities and which you now find to be only a hundred yards or so farther down the road.

Having chosen or found your camp site, what then? First, call at the office, which is always near the entrance, and book in. The warden will give you a receipt – I always pin this on my tent as it saves his looking for me when he makes his daily round. If you are abroad, the warden will ask to see your passport and may retain it (you can leave your Camping Carnet, if you have one, in place of your passport). He may also give you a form to complete; this is the same form as that which a hotelier asks his guests to fill up.

Remember to read the rules which are always posted on the warden's office. These are certain to include such points as not disturbing the hours of silence, which as a rule are between 10.00 p.m. and 6.00 a.m.; not digging drains on the site; not lighting fires; not damaging trees by hammering in nails – in order to hang up washing, for example; controlling dogs, if they are allowed on the site; and the use of radios with consideration to others. If, however, you follow the "Camping Code", which is printed at the end of this book, you will not go wrong.

Well, you have booked in! What next? Only use the pitch which has been allocated to you by the warden. His directions may be quite specific, such as "Use pitch number 23", and if this is the case that is the pitch you must use. But even in such a strictly regulated site he will generally let you choose your pitch as far as he is able. A more usual direction is on the lines of "Anywhere at the end of the field". In this case you pitch where you like, subject to a few common-sense rules which I will discuss in the next chapter.

Leaving the Site

There is no problem here – pack up and ensure that no trace of your stay remains. If you have left your Camping Carnet or your passport at the office, collect it. In any case, it does no harm to say goodbye and then, if it is appropriate, thank the warden. He usually merits your thanks.

Animals in Camp

I know from letters in the camping magazines that my comments will be most unpopular with many readers, but I am strongly against animals (by which I really mean dogs) in camp. Naturally, I am aware that all dog owners consider their pets to be well behaved and well trained, and are convinced that they – the owners themselves – always maintain good order and discipline as far as their particular animals are concerned. In theory, all sites admitting pets insist – at least according to their notices and literature – on the animal being kept in order. This all very well, but my experience is that most dogs go almost completely unchecked. Because there are no lamp-posts, tents are soiled and so is the grass. I have been kept awake by a dog whining to get out and another yapping to get in, and where there is more than one dog on the site they cause considerable noise both late at night and early in the morning. Some of them steal food from open tents and damage closed tents looking for food they can smell.

I am aware that I am classing all dogs and dog owners together and that this is very unfair, but sufficient are of

the type I have described for me to say quite definitely –
"no dogs in camp!". If you are a prospective camper and
also a dog owner, do not allow my comments to worry you
unduly. The majority of sites accept you and your pet; but
please, please do not allow it to disturb other campers.

Whilst on the subject of dogs, I would like to mention
some little corner protectors I noticed near some tents
recently. They were about a foot high and exactly like
miniature windshields – made of tent fabric and three
posts. The posts were sharpened and dug into the ground
about six inches from each corner of the tent. On enquiry,
I was told that these shields protect the tent from dogs who
like to use the corners as lavatories. They appeared to work
successfully and might be worth trying if you have suffered
from this misfortune.

Chapter 22

Pitches and Pitching

Requirements for the perfect pitch are so many that a glance through the list would discourage you, or might even put you off camping for ever. But it is not really as bad as that, so let us have a look at what we need for perfection:

1. A level pitch.
2. A pitch free of stones or roots which might damage the groundsheet.
3. A dry pitch.
4. Shelter from the prevailing wind.
5. In hot climates or weather, shelter from the direct sun in the heat of the day.
6. The pitch should be sheltered by trees, but the tent should not be placed directly under them.
7. Not too near to the next tent.
8. Not too close to the toilets or entrance.
9. Depending on how lazy you feel, a pitch reasonably far from the water point, shops, etc.
10. A firm approach and parking space for your car.

Perhaps some of these "necessities" require further explanation, so I will take them one by one.

1 Level

Remember that water runs down a slope and that in a storm rain water can actually run through a tent. Old-timers used to dig small ditches round their tents to run the water away, but this is not allowed on an organized site (the mess at the end of the season if everyone dug their own private ditches can well be imagined). Another point to bear in mind is that camp beds tip over if placed across a slope, and you will roll off an air bed. If you place the bed so that your head is downhill, you will find it most uncomfortable (should you have no choice but to pitch on a slope, at least make sure that you can sleep with your head higher than your feet). Tables, unless provided with telescopic legs, will try hard – and usually succeed – to slide your crockery onto the ground when placed on a slope. You cannot, of course, erect a frame tent correctly on a slope, for not only will the frame itself tend to twist but also the fabric will be stretched in some places and loose in others. The tension naturally causes damage, and so does slackness as the wind catches and hammers at loose canvas, causing a surprising amount of stretching. It is seldom that a tent badly damaged in this way recovers. Try hard to find a level pitch; it is well worth it.

The motor caravanner is also concerned to find level ground on which to park his vehicle. If he parks off the level, his water will not run and he may find that he has trouble with his gas; dishes will slide off the cooker and table and, if the slope is very severe, he may even roll out of bed. Neither the caravanner nor the trailer tent owner is unduly worried by a slight slope as he is able to level his 'van or trailer with the jacks provided. But he would still be unwise to park on too steep a slope.

2. *Free of stones or roots*

This is a matter of lengthening the life of your expensive tent. Should you be using a small tent and sleeping on the ground, stones and roots can be very uncomfortable, but more important is the damage that can be done to your frame tent. Sewn-in groundsheets are very strong, considering how thin they are, and withstand heavy wear, but they are nonetheless susceptible to cuts by stones and roots. Similarly, air beds are punctured by the sharp edges of stones and roots. The former should always be moved and the latter avoided. Both, of course, make it impossible to drive your tent pegs into the ground, thereby making pitching quite a problem.

3 *A dry pitch*

This speaks for itself. I am not referring to surface moisture, which is only to be expected after rain, but rather to the type of ground that floods or turns into a bog after rain. If you select level ground, you should not have much to worry about. Avoid gullies and hollows, and areas of lush green grass which, although they may appear most attractive in dry weather, can indicate marshy conditions or perhaps an underground spring. Try to visualise the ground after heavy rain. If what appears to be a first-class pitching area is avoided by the rest of the campers, it is as well to find out why before dashing off to put your tent right in the middle of it.

A dry pitch is equally important for the caravanner and motor caravanner. Whilst these campers are not worried by rain or the occasional puddle, they are likely to wake up or return to camp to find their vehicles well and truly bogged down if they park on marshy ground. Also remember that the jacks used for levelling caravans will sink into soft ground and cause considerable difficulty and even damage to the 'van.

4, 5 and 6 *Shelter from the wind and sun*

Shelter from the wind is mainly a matter of common sense. In windy areas or at any time when a gale may be expected, it is as well to pitch in a spot which is protected from the prevailing wind. Incidentally, a tent should always be pitched with its back to the wind, as this prevents draughts through the door and the wind from getting underneath and lifting the awning. A wall, building, group of trees or even a hedge make useful windbreaks. If you must pitch in the open, you can use your car to break the wind. I have used additional guys from the top of the tent to the roof rack of a car. If you do use the car for additional security, do not forget to unhitch before you drive off – I am sure a car towing its tent behind it would be a source of great amusement, but it would also cause considerable and expensive damage to the tent.

In very hot weather or in hot countries abroad, it is sensible to ensure that you have some shade from the midday sun – the inside of an unprotected tent can become very hot indeed. As a rule, the only things which provide shade from the sun are buildings or trees, and because, as campers, we usually attempt to avoid buildings this leaves trees. Use the trees to give shade but not direct cover. If you site your tent or 'van carefully, you will find it is possible to pitch in a position such that you are not directly underneath the trees but they provide shade. There are several reasons why the trees, should be a little way away from your tent. Boughs can break off and fall upon the tent and its occupants. Birds can be a nuisance; they perch in the trees over the tent and the result can be a nasty mess on the roof fabric, even after quite a short time. Insects gather under trees and cause noise and annoying, and sometimes painful, bites in the evening. The leaves of some trees produce a gum which drops onto the fabric, and they also collect dust and dirt which is washed off by the rain and falls on the tent or caravan beneath. Finally, trees will drip water long after it has stopped raining.

7 *Not too close to the next tent*

It is common sense and plain good manners not to pitch too near to someone else's tent. I am always very annoyed when I return to the site to find a tent pitched so close to mine that the guy lines are crossing each other. Other than being bad manners, pitching so close means that you receive the benefit of his radio and he yours – and any other noise from the tent, such as crying children or barking dogs. Remember also that your neighbour may well use his car battery for tent lighting and will need to bring his car close up to his tent; he will not be pleased if you have blocked his way.

In Europe, it is the custom to mark off the car space next to your tent with string when you are leaving camp. I have done this in England at a Bank Holiday, using my string of pennants as a rope and putting up a polite notice – no one objected or pitched on the space. Similarly, it is by no means unusual to see a simple notice to the effect that "this pitch is occupied by motor caravan no. . . .". If you have a motor caravan, you will naturally want to use the vehicle as a car and it is extremely annoying to arrive back from a sightseeing trip to find that your pitch has been taken by newcomers. When marking out the space occupied by your car or motor caravan, do use neat posts and, preferably, coloured cord; site owners do not like to see ugly fences erected by their campers.

8 and 9 *Not too close to the toilets, entrance, camp shop or water point*

You may think it convenient to be pitched near the camp entrance and toilets. Being near the latter may sound a particularly good idea, especially if you have small children and the water point is in the toilet block. However, this is the noisiest part of the camp; there is a fairly constant stream of visitors to the toilet during the day and, if there is any movement in the site at all at night, it centres on this particular building. As far as the entrance is concerned, most sites are protected by a gate, and cars draw to a halt, wait while somebody gets out and opens the gate, and then pull away – this is repeated as the gate has to be closed. Of course, the doors of the cars are banged twice at each side of the gate every time someone enters or leaves camp. At night the noise is similar, except that it is much more noticeable and is accompanied by the glare of headlamps. My opinion is that it is better to keep away from these parts of the site and find a quieter pitch.

Very much the same applies to the camp shop and water point. If you are too close, you will have the same stream of campers to-ing and fro-ing past your tent. It is amazing how some people will actually walk over your guy lines to avoid walking an extra yard or so. On the other hand, a 2-gallon carrier of water weighs 20 lbs and takes quite a bit of carrying; shopping can also be heavy. You have therefore to strike a balance between finding a quiet pitch and having to carry your shopping and water quite a distance, and the lazy life accompanied by noise. I would advise the former; walking is part of a camping holiday and carrying hurt no man unless he was infirm or aged. The ideal set-up, of course, is to pitch well away from the facilities and leave all the carrying to your wife, but this depends on whether or not you think you can get away with it.

10 *Firm approach and parking space for cars*

It is very easy to drive onto a site on a perfect evening, park the car on the selected pitch and put up the tent only to wake up the next morning to find that it has rained heavily and your car wheels just spin on the wet and possibly muddy ground. This can happen to the most careful of us, especially when we drive onto a rather crowded site and find very little choice of pitch, or onto a site where the pitches are numbered and allocated. The latter are rare in this country, but are frequently to be found in southern Europe. If you are cautious, you should not have too much trouble. Do not select hollows, watch for lush green grass of the type which thrives on dampness and avoid gullies which would turn into watercourses in a storm. If you see marks in the grass which indicate that the previous camper has had trouble moving his car, keep clear. The corner stays of a caravan or trailer tent will dig into soft ground and may upset the balance of the 'van or trailer. A good many caravan parks have concrete pieces for parking 'vans and these are usually on level ground – or at least the concrete is level – which saves a great deal of trouble.

Never leave your car parked on a slope, facing up or down hill, relying solely on your handbrake. At least leave it in gear or, better still, park it sideways across the hill. Cars have been known to run away down slopes with fatal results.

If a little common sense and observation is used, no camper, however inexperienced, should have any trouble. This applies to all aspects of camping. Perhaps, by listing ten points to avoid and describing each one at length, I have tended to frighten off the prospective newcomers to camping. I sincerely hope that this is not the case as I have seldom seen anyone really in trouble, although I have seen some very dirty tents and caravans as the result of pitching under trees. In any case, campers are a friendly bunch and no one is in difficulties for very long without being surrounded by a band of helpful volunteers.

Tent Repairs on the Site

In Chapter 10 I have discussed looking after, repairing and storing a tent in some detail, and also stressed the importance of inspecting your tent for damage when breaking camp for the last time of the season and making early repairs ready for next year's holiday. Your tent should therefore be in good condition on arrival at the site and, provided that you erect it correctly on a good pitch, able to withstand severe weather conditions. However, accidents can happen and there will doubtless be occasions when you have to make some on-the-spot repairs.

Accidents invariably result from carelessness. For example, the inadvertent use of anything sharp, such as a peg or stick, can tear the canvas, and a badly put together frame may bend in a strong wind – or even give way completely. Let me briefly describe some of the emergency repairs that you might find yourself forced to make.

Should the fabric tear, cut a patch to fit the rent from spare tent material or canvas and stick it over the tear with one of the impact glues. Follow the instructions on the glue carefully as you require its maximum strength. Once the patch is on and dry, stitch the edges of the tear to the patch. It is advisable to turn the tent so that the repaired tear is away from the wind. Torn plastic windows can be repaired with a piece of polythene stuck on with impact adhesive.

Although it is always best to replace a bent section of the frame, a replacement will rarely be available locally. In this case, you should gently straighten out the damaged section, trying hard not to flatten the tube where the bend occurred. If the section does tend to flatten, you may be able to restore it to a reasonable shape by placing it on a raised, flat object – for instance, a tree stump – and tapping it with your tent mallet. There will be no strength in the section at all if it is left flat where it bent.

Should you have to replace a guy line, use nylon cord. If you have to thread it through a small hole or tunnel in the canvas, it helps to hold the end in the heat from a gas cooker or even a match. This seals the threads together and prevents them from spreading out as you try to thread the cord through the hole.

As soon as possible, have professional repairs made so that you are ready for your next camping trip.

Chapter 23

Food and Cooking in Camp

Meals are an important part of any holiday and a camping holiday is no exception, but it is essential that no undue strain should be put on the cook, who is usually mother. Everyone should take his or her turn so that your trip is a holiday for all the family. Try to avoid any set routine exported from home, especially if it is complicated. I think you will save time and trouble if you buy a few pieces of special equipment. I have discussed cooking utensils and the various types of stoves available in Chapters 6 and 7 respectively. But I think you will find that a gas stove gives the least trouble, and I would also recommend that you invest in one of the mini pressure cookers which double as a saucepan.

We find it convenient to arrive at our chosen site with all our necessities packed in airtight plastic boxes or jars. These contain just about everything – salt, sugar, butter and cooking fat, jam, marmalade, tea, coffee and powdered milk. We take packets of soup, but powdered potatoes, cornflakes and even meat are carried in plastic containers.

We live or exist on three meals a day in camp. Breakfast is my favourite meal of the day – in fact, we have no anti-breakfast people in the family, perhaps because we are all non-smokers. Lunch is usually a scratch meal, taken at odd times to fit in with trips or even eaten en route. Supper, however, is another "main meal".

The important thing is to avoid monotony. Nothing is

more likely to put your wife and children off camping than a fortnight of fried food or cornflakes. This is such an easy trap to fall into. A normal camp cooking outfit consists of a nesting set of three billies for boiling with lids which are used as frying pans. You therefore have three frying pans to hand, and frying is quick and uses little gas.

Although my family like nice food we do not bother with elaborate dishes. We believe in eating the local foods and therefore buy as we are attracted by shop window or market displays. As a precaution, we buy a stock of tinned or dehydrated foods on arrival or on the way to our site. If we are going abroad, we take our reserve or emergency supply with us.

Breakfast can consist of a cereal followed by boiled eggs and bread and butter, or if, like me, you are ambitious you can fry potatoes (reconstituted powder), sausages, hamburgers, eggs or anything else fryable. Toast is difficult, but very often you can obtain fresh rolls in time for breakfast, and with them you have butter and marmalade, or jam, or honey.

Lunch can be a restaurant meal should you be in a town, or if you are on "safari" you can cook a quick meal quite easily without carrying a great deal of your gear. Reconstituted packet soup can be cooked on a small, solid-fuel cooker which you can carry in your pocket. When you cook a packet soup, add a tablespoonful of powdered milk – it is a great improvement. Diced bread added to the soup makes a filling meal. If you are still hungry, you can fill up on chocolate or fruit.

For supper you can have soup – if you do not have it for lunch. If you possess a pressure cooker, you are able to serve up a great variety of meals – different meats, poultry, vegetables, etc. Without such an exotic piece of equipment you are left with your billies to heat up tinned meats and puddings, but there are many kinds to choose from. To finish up you have an infinite choice of fruit. Custard is easy to make: you simply add one and a half tablespoonfuls of powdered milk to custard powder and pour on boiling water.

We use powdered milk a lot. It is easy to carry and there is no problem of its turning sour. Without a 'fridge, fresh milk will not keep in the summer and must therefore be used immediately it is obtained. This is usually possible for the breakfast cereal. If there is a near-by stream, we use it as a "fridge" (milk will keep well in running water), propping the bottle upright with a couple of stones, but otherwise powdered milk is our answer. There are many brands on the market and these fall into two main types: some have the fat content removed and are first-class in coffee; others have the animal fat extracted and vegetable fat added. Which is best is a matter of opinion. Try several brands and come to your own conclusion. You can, of course, get all sorts of other drinks in easy-to-carry packs, including tea, coffee, Horlicks, cocoa and Ovaltine.

These easy-to-carry packs are very useful to lightweight campers, to whom minimum weight is of great importance. In a party I helped to organise recently each boy carried a rucksack weighing less than 30 lbs, which included food for five days. The expedition was to last four days, but an extra day's ration was carried to allow for emergencies. Each boy took a change of underwear, three pairs of thick socks, a sleeping bag, personal toilet gear and eating irons. Naturally, each also carried a torch, map, compass and whistle. Tent, groundsheets, cooking stoves and utensils were shared between the boys working in small groups. A first-aid kit was also shared by each group. All food, such as cereal, coffee, tea, sugar and so on, was shared and as far as possible carried loose in plastic bags in order to fit into the smallest possible space. As this was an expedition, specially packed meat bars were used, as were filling biscuits of the wholemeal type. Powdered soup, vegetables and potatoes, and lemonade in crystal form were also carried. Weight was our main consideration. As I have said before, most foods are available in dehydrated form nowadays, and in addition the party took fruit-flavoured glucose, nuts and raisins, bacon (which keeps well) and dried apple flakes. Porridge was a great filler. Water, duly sterilised with tablets, was taken from streams or pumps in villages.

When camping, especially on the Continent, you will probably find that your biggest item of expense is food – more so if you make regular use of restaurants. Many of my friends take large quantities of tinned and preserved food with them, but unless you know in advance the price of individual items available in the country to which you are going I do not think this helps. Why lumber yourself with stacks of tins only to find that they could have been bought at the same price locally? The one exception I would make to this is when you have young children with you. They tend to dislike anything which is not familiar to them, so it is a good idea to take a few packets of a well-known cereal and a limited number of other items. Older children should be encouraged to try local foods.

If you are intending to "eat out", it will be far cheaper to do so at restaurants in side streets rather than at the well-known ones in the centre of town. You may not get the same spotless table linen and you might have to take soup with a dessert spoon, but you will pay far less for the same food. How much luxury you should sacrifice for economy

is naturally a matter of opinion and everybody must decide
for himself or herself.

A common source of extravagance when camping
abroad is to buy more than is required whilst shopping in
local markets; this is because most shoppers tend to regard
a kilo as two pounds. I agree that this makes life easier, but
as a result you end up with more food than you actually
need or would use at home, and this mounts up over a
period of a couple of weeks. I admit that by treating a litre
as two pints the reverse takes place, but you will be buying
more solid food than drink.

Talking about drink, I find that water is a subject which
worries many holidaymakers. You find two completely
opposite schools of thought when you discuss drinking
water with campers. Some declare that they drink water
straight from the tap "with never a spot of bother", whilst
others sterilise or boil all water and tell dreadful tales of
tummy troubles. As in most cases when two sets of opinions are so far apart, I suppose the truth is somewhere in
between. I tend to consider that most mains tap water is all
right, but still prefer to put sterilising tablets in water that
is to be used for drinking, cooking or washing up. As a
result, we have never had any trouble. Some people say
sterilised water has an unpleasant taste, but I do not find
this is so. We always keep our container full of "clean"
water and in this way we have had no trouble. Every time
your container is half empty, re-fill it.

You can sterilize your water by boiling it – which is rather
extravagant on your fuel and can be expensive if you use
gas – or with special tablets obtainable from all chemists.
There is also a filtering outfit on the market. Which, if any,
of these methods you use is better decided for yourself.

Many of the leading food manufacturers supply cook

books either written specially or suitable for campers. These are sold at very reasonable prices – sometimes they are free – and are well worth obtaining.

Finally, two tips which I think helpful. The first is, never put fuel in food bottles or containers, even if they are clearly labelled. Remember that small children cannot read, and that those who can tend to drink first and read later. The second is that it is unwise to warm up food cooked on a previous occasion. Even if the food is left in airtight containers, bacteria can enter before the bottle or jar is sealed and then multiply. In some cases, re-heating will not destroy them, so it may well be better to eat late and safely than to eat early on a re-heated meal and suffer as a result.

Chapter 24

Dangers in Camp

I do not wish to emphasise the dangers which are present when camping, but I think they ought to be mentioned for the benefit of newcomers to the camping family. I will not discuss those accidents which can occur on all types of holiday, except to say that cuts, broken limbs and shock are always possible because the young, and old for that matter, will attempt climbs and so on which are clearly too ambitious for them. It is always dangerous to attempt rock climbs unless you are sufficiently knowledgeable to appreciate the dangers, especially those of the descent, and it is very unwise to explore caves and potholes unless properly equipped and guided.

Campers using tents, and to a lesser extent caravans, face two dangers in particular which are appreciated by far too few of us; these are fire and bites.

1 Fire

The usual causes of a fire in camp are careless cooking, equally careless lighting, and spilling oil or petrol whilst filling liquid fuel stoves and lamps in the tent. As far as I am aware, there is only one make of tent which is flame-proof. If it fulfils your requirements, you may be advised to buy it; if it is not exactly what you want, you must weigh up the advantages and disadvantages and decide for yourself. Several makes of tent have plastic-lined kitchen extensions which not only allow grease to be washed off but also provide a reasonable amount of fireproofing. If you are cooking in a tent, especially in a low tent, remember that fat in a frying pan can catch fire and throw flames up quite high; your tent will vanish in seconds should the flames reach the side walls or roof. It is unwise to cook in a frame tent whilst people are zipped up inside the sleeping compartments.

As far as lighting is concerned, the danger arises from the careless use of liquid fuel. It is only too easy to spill fuel when filling stoves and lamps, and this can result in a flame running along the spilt fuel to a tent wall. Draughts can also cause a sudden flare-up with a lamp which may result in a fire.

Fire is always a nasty thing, but particularly so in a tent. It takes very little contact with a flame to set canvas alight, then there is a roar and the tent goes up like a petrol explosion. Once alight it is hard to put out, even if there is time. In a wind a tent can become an inferno within seconds. What can be done to avoid starting a fire? The danger can be reduced to almost nil by taking a few simple and common-sense precautions.

First, before leaving home check up on your cooking and lighting equipment. Cooking and fire risk go together; if you use liquid fuel, check all your equipment, containers, washers and screw threads. If you use gas, check all connecting tubes and the taps.

Never cook in camp with any curtains or hangings near the flame; never adjust the container or connection when the apparatus is working, or when you have another cooker or lamp working in the tent or caravan; do not remove a disposable container before it is empty in an enclosed space, such as a tent or caravan; do not store spare liquid fuel or gas containers in your tent or caravan.

Some motorists have a fire extinquisher. If you own one, keep it in a handy place in camp; if you do not, consider purchasing one at once. Even if you cannot get at it should you have a fire in your tent, it is available for use by someone else, or for you to use should some other unfortunate person have a fire in his tent.

Finally, let me repeat that if you take due care and precautions the risk is very slight – and it is up to you.

I have no doubt greatly exaggerated the danger in order to make my point, but I know of two tents which vanished in what was little more than a flash of flame, severely burning the occupants. As I have said, there is very little danger indeed if common sense is used. But you have only to walk round a camping site to see the careless risks taken with naked flames, and it is to such people and the uninformed beginner that I address this section. It is only fair to say that very few campers, even of years standing, have ever seen a tent fire and this also applies to site owners; there is only danger if you put it there yourself.

2 Bites

Whilst insects can cause uncomfortable and even painful bites, these are usually treated successfully with proprietary remedies. Your local chemist or doctor will advise you if necessary. There are, however, still places in this country where adders are found and a bite from this snake requires immediate treatment, especially in the case of a child. Snakes are just as frightened of you as you are of them and the danger arises when you scare or tread on them. If you are in adder country, the danger is slight if you have a sewn-in groundsheet, and on an organised site where the grass is short the danger is non-existent. It is the lone lightweight camper who pitches in isolated and wild places who may encounter an adder. Although an adder bite is unlikely to be fatal, except perhaps to a small child, immediate medical attention should be obtained if you are bitten. The snake is dark in colour with a "V" marking behind its head. It may well be 2 ft or more long.

3 Fumes from Dry Cleaning

There has been comment in the camping press about the danger of fumes from recently cleaned sleeping bags. If your sleeping bag is dirty, have it cleaned well before you will require it again so that it can be thoroughly aired. If your bag does not zip fully open, turn it inside out and hang it up for a reasonable time.

4 Ultra-lightweight Blankets

I understand that it can be dangerous to put your head under some types of ultra-lightweight blankets, the effect being much the same as putting your head in a plastic bag. I have not experimented myself, but think this should be considered when using these blankets on children's beds. They are certainly wonderfully warm, although if you are a restless sleeper they can be somewhat noisy as they tend to crackle.

Chapter 25

Exposure

Exposure is caused by exhaustion and the chilling of the surface of the body, usually in rain and wind. Typical signs that a person is suffering from exposure are complaints that he is cold or tired, attacks of cramp and abnormal behaviour, such as failure to understand conversation and suggestions. His speech may become slurred and he may be unable to focus properly. In fact, watch for any unusual or unexplained behaviour. The final symptoms are collapse and coma.

To avoid exposure wear good windproof and rainproof clothing, and avoid getting overtired. Worry and mental strain often contribute to exposure, so keep the party cheerful and give plenty of encouragement. Ensure that the weaker members of the party are not forced by fear of adverse comment to overdo things; you must never, never make fun of the slower ones. Regular meals, which should include energy providing foods, are essential. If any member of the party shows the slightest sign of exposure, stop at once in a sheltered place. If after a rest and a hot drink he still appears abnormal, ignore such statements as "I'll be all right, I'll carry on" – be cautious and get him to a doctor. The leader must make a great effort to ensure that the remainder of the party are not reduced to the same condition.

An exposure victim must be treated at once as his condition can rapidly worsen. I repeat, as soon as you suspect exposure, stop immediately in a sheltered spot and put up a tent or bivouac, allowing the patient plenty of rest and preventing further loss of heat. Protection from the cold rising from the ground is vital. It is also advisable to cover the head, face and neck. Heat can be provided by placing a warm companion in the bivouac with him. Certainly supply hot food and drink; the latter should include sugar, glucose and condensed milk. Never rub the victim to restore circulation, give alcohol or allow any movement which would use up more energy. If there is no sign of breathing, apply mouth-to-mouth resuscitation.

If there are three people in the party, one can go for help whilst the other remains with the exposure victim. If there are only two, it may be necessary to leave him alone. Should you be carrying a lightweight tent, no doubt you will use this, but if you are not the answer is to make the "Hedgecoe" bivi with two groundsheets. Even if you do have a tent, I think the bivi is more suitable for an exposure victim. It is easy to make, as you will see from the illustrations, and even in rain you will see steam rising

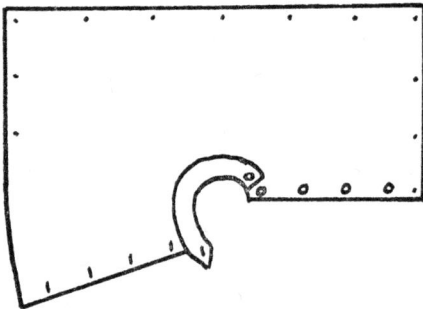

Fig. 98

from the upper groundsheet showing how much heat is being produced inside.

As a rule, campers and walkers carry a square civilian groundsheet, but I think that the army type, which has a flap and can be worn as a cape or turned into a tent (this requires two sheets), is much better. Certainly the flap is useful if you use the groundsheet to make a bivi (see Fig. 98). As well as two groundsheets, you require a

Fig. 99 Double peg for strength.

"bivi-pole" (see Fig. 99), a dozen skewer-type tent pegs and 6 ft of cord. Cord is usually carried as an emergency measure and there is no reason why the two 12-in sections of pole should not be tucked down a pack. The sleeve which joins the two sections of pole can be made from a food tin with both ends cut out.

When erecting the bivi, it is essential to form a windproof and rainproof seal down the closed side and end. The windproof corner always faces the wind. To form the seal the groundsheets are laid out on top of each other and the pegs are inserted down one side. Next the sheets are turned over so that a windproof tuck is formed, the tops of the pegs now being concealed by the sheets. The sealed end is made by putting pegs through the holes the wrong way and then turning in the end of the material. Now the pegs can be pushed into the ground. As the heads of the pegs are covered by two layers of groundsheet, do not use a mallet – this will tear the material.

Now button up the flap of one groundsheet to the other and run your cord through the holes of the two groundsheets, taking it to the peg which can be seen in the illustration. The bivi-pole is pushed through the hole in the groundsheet and the base is rested on the ground (not on the lower groundsheet). Once you are inside, you can seal yourself away from the outside by pulling the cord tight. This also lifts up the lower edge of the bottom ground-sheet and prevents rain from running in. Kit can be placed at the head of the bivouac to form a pillow. Fig. 100 shows this type of home-made bivi.

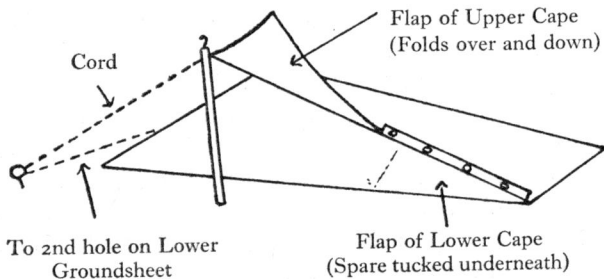

Fig. 100

The main advantage of the bivi is that it takes up much less space than a tent, both in the pack and when on the ground. Admittedly the occupant cannot stretch out at full length when inside, but most people sleep curled up.

A two-man bivouac can be formed by making two bivis end to end with the flaps of the two top groundsheets over-lapped. The occupants sleep head to head.

It is worth having a last look at the ideal site for a light-weight tent or shelter. The requirements are:

1. Shelter from the north and prevailing wind.
2. A flat area for the actual bivi or tent, but with a slight overall slope to run off surface water.
3. A supply of drinking water near by.

4. A stream or lake for washing and washing up. Of course, this may also be the drinking water supply.
5. If required, a supply of dry fuel for cooking or warmth.

Avoid low-lying or marshy ground, be suspicious of lush green grass and avoid deep woods – they are damp and insect ridden.

Bedding-down

Always have a groundsheet beneath your bedding, even in dry weather on dry ground. If you do not have a sleeping bag, overlap the blankets as shown in Fig. 101 (note the use of your coat or anorak). A

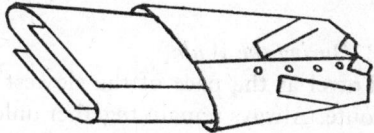

Fig. 101

layer of heather or bracken can be placed beneath the groundsheet for comfort and warmth.

Clothing should always be loosened to avoid constricting the circulation; this maintains warmth. The bootlaces, waistband, belt and anything tight at the neck should be undone.

Safety Precautions for Lightweight Campers

A *Preparation*

1. Carry a map, compass, whistle, first-aid kit and torch.
2. Carry spare warm clothing.
3. Carry emergency rations, which should not be touched except in the event of an emergency.

4. Ensure that someone knows of your route and anticipated time of arrival.
5. Decide on your drill should any member of the party get lost – for example, "walk north until you reach the main road".
6. Do not wear too heavy clothing or carry too much kit.

Naturally, your route should be planned in advance and the weather conditions considered.

Before you leave, the leader should check the equipment of each member of the party.

B *During the Walk*

Travel at the pace of the slowest man and stick to your route. Always remain together unless you have a casualty, in which case he should not be left alone. This is why a party should not be less than four or five strong.

Should the party get lost, do not split up or panic – use your map and compass. If the weather turns bad you should always turn back, or stop and camp.

C *The Causes of Accidents*

Most accidents in open or mountainous country are caused by carelessness, over-confidence in one's own physical or technical ability, failure of the party to work together, lack of knowledge and observation, lack of proper kit and mere failure to use common sense. Remember that it is often better to take a longer route than a much shorter but difficult one.

Appendices

Appendix A

Camping Periodicals and Clubs

I do not think it would be of much value to the reader merely to list the camping magazines and clubs, so I propose to say a few words about each of those mentioned. The magazines are well worth buying. All contain readers' comments on sites and articles on tours, tents, caravans, motor caravans and camping equipment, as well as giving tips on maintenance and service. Although I suppose that over a period they must cover very much the same ground, I have read them with great interest for many years – several, in fact, since they were first published.

I am a member of the Camping Club of Great Britain and Ireland and the Auto Camping Club and speak from experience about these. As far as the other clubs are concerned, I have taken extracts from the literature which they very kindly supplied to me. I have avoided mentioning prices, subscriptions and so on as these tend to change – mostly, I am afraid, in an ever upward direction.

Periodicals

Camping. Published on the 6th of the month by Caravan Publications Ltd., Link House, Dingwell Avenue, Croydon, Surrey. This magazine covers all aspects of tent, motor caravan, trailer tent camping and caravanning.

Caravan. Published on the 25th of the month. Touring, trailer caravanning and motor caravans. Published by Caravan Publications Ltd., Link House, Dingwell Avenue, Croydon, Surrey.

Practical Camper. Published monthly by the Haymarket Press, 5 Winsley Street, London W.1. A magazine covering tent and trailer tent camping, and caravanning.

Practical Caravan. Published monthly by the Haymarket Press, 5 Winsley Street, London W.1. This is a companion magazine to the *Practical Camper*, and caters for the touring trailer caravan and motor caravan owner.

Motor Caravan and Camping. This magazine is concerned with every type of camping – tents, trailer tents, trailer caravans and motor caravans – and thus is of interest to all campers. It is also the official magazine of the Auto Camping club, whose members are able to purchase it at a considerably reduced price.

There are other magazines on the market, but the above are the ones which I find most interesting, informative and readable.

Camping and Caravan Clubs

There are several clubs, some of which, like the Camping Club of Great Britain and Ireland and the Auto Camping Club, cater for all types of camper, including motor caravanners and trailer caravanners. The Auto Camping Club presses for the unity of all campers and the opening of sites to all without segregation.

THE CAMPING CLUB OF GREAT BRITAIN AND IRELAND

11 Lower Grosvenor Place, London S.W.1.

With over 100 000 members, the Camping Club speaks with authority for British campers.

Throughout the country, the Club's district associations and sections arrange camping weeks, weekend camps, holiday tours, social events and a host of outdoor activities.

The Club itself owns or administers many excellent sites – some of the best of them exclusive to members. These sites are in beauty spots and near holiday resorts – on the coast, by river, lake or mountain.

The Club's many sections cater for a wide variety of special interests – canoeing, climbing, cycling, caravanning (both trailer and motor), trailer tents, folk dancing and photography – all sections have their own full programmes of activities and provide their members with services of many kinds.

For overseas touring, membership is of great benefit. The Club has reciprocal arrangements with many foreign camping clubs under which our members receive the facilities these clubs give their own members. The Club is prominent in "Campers International", the Federation Internationale de Camping et Caravanning. It has a valuable international touring service, including the issue of the International Camping Carnet and an excellent annual international sites list.

The Club's high prestige has enabled it to secure for its members an exemption from the restrictive provisions and legislation of the Public Health Act (1936), the Town and Country Planning Act (1947) and the Caravan Sites Control and Development Act (1960). Members are able to use these privileges under conditions laid down by the Club's National Council.

To sum up, I list just a few of the main benefits of membership:

1. A free monthly illustrated magazine.
2. A yearbook and annually revised list of some 2500 inspected sites.
3. Use of the Club's own sites widely spread through the country.
4. Cheap insurance facilities (including vehicle insurance at reduced rates) and substantial free kit insurance.
5. A foreign tourist service backed by expert knowledge.
6. A free technical handbook.

The Club's magazine *Camping and Outdoor Life* is not obtainable from booksellers; it is issued to members only. It is a first-class publication, the contents ranging over all aspects of camping.

With its huge membership and associated clubs and sections, the Camping Club exerts considerable influence on local authorities. All campers, no matter what type of camping they favour, should join and add power to the efforts of the Club.

Constant vigilance is needed to ensure that access to the countryside and freedom to camp are not unduly restricted. The Club keeps an ever-watchful eye on the camper's interests at parliamentary and local levels. A growing number of M.P.s of all parties are members of the Club.

The Club co-operates with other bodies to preserve our country's natural beauties. It works with other organisations to foster many outdoor activities. Government departments, local authorities and such bodies as the

Forestry Commission and National Parks Commission frequently ask the Club's advice.

THE AUTO CAMPING CLUB
51a Chipstead Valley Road, Coulsdon, Surrey

The Club was formed to bring together all tent and trailer campers, caravanners and motor caravanners.

The Auto Camping Club claims that it is not in opposition but complementary to all existing clubs, and aims to unite campers and caravanners so that they may speak with one voice to all authority.

Objects of the Club

1. To unite all campers, caravanners and motor caravanners, and the organisations catering for them.
2. To further and protect the interests of all campers and caravanners.
3. To encourage the development of all forms of camping and caravanning.
4. To establish and maintain high standards of conduct in all campers and caravanners.
5. To hold exhibitions, rallies, meetings and displays.
6. To preserve the countryside and access thereto of all campers and caravanners.
7. To find or provide sites and night halts for all campers and caravanners.

Membership offers you:

(a) Use of the Club's advisory service on all matters concerning all forms of camping and caravanning.
(b) Concessional insurance facilities.

(c) Discounts on equipment.

(d) The companionship of other campers and caravanners at rallies, meetings and social events.

(e) Home and overseas touring service.

(f) The Club's official magazine *Motor Caravan and Camping* and other associated publications at reduced prices. (It is not, incidentally, a condition of the Club that members take the official magazine.)

THE CANOE CAMPING CLUB
(Section of the Camping Club of Great Britain and Ireland)
11 Lower Grosvenor Place, London S.W.1.

Canoe camping gives you liberty, freedom of expression and healthy relaxation. You are only half alive to the wonders of nature if you have never canoed along a quiet river towards the setting sun; you have missed the good life if you have never travelled by canal, river, lake and sea. Canoe camping offers fun afloat for the whole family; it enables one to explore where no other craft can penetrate. Anywhere in the world a member of the Canoe Camping Club is bound to make friends because a canoe makes introductions easy yet affords solitude and adventure.

The Canoe Camping Club is the largest nation-wide canoe club and has regional groups throughout Britain. Membership entitles you to:

1. All the facilities of the Camping Club

2. Free monthly magazine *Camping and Outdoor Life* and quarterly magazine *The Canoe Camper*.

3. Free camping kit insurance and canoe insurance at the Club's special rates.

4. Free 136-page *Handbook of Camping*, listing some 3500 selected camping sites and indicating those with access to water.

5. Exclusive Camping Club sites.

6. Foreign tourist service.

7. A large and comprehensive library of books on canoeing and camping.

8. Discounts at selected camp kit and canoe suppliers.

9. Use of the Club's boathouse at Chertsey.

10. Free advice on solo touring.

11. Use of the Club's Norfolk Broads licences.

12. Technical advice on canoe design and construction, inland and sea touring, racing and slalom.

13. Guidance and advice for beginners.

14. Information on canoeing waters at home and abroad.

Organised national tours are held at Easter, Whitsun and during the summer. Regional groups arrange weekend and day runs, films, lectures and discussions.

THE BRITISH CARAVANNERS CLUB
11 Lower Grosvenor Place, London S.W.1.

The British Caravanners Club was formed as the Caravan Section of the Camping Club of Great Britain and Ireland (with over 100 000 members), and as such has much influence in camping and caravanning matters throughout the country.

Membership of the British Caravanners Club entitles you to the following:

1. Membership of the Camping Club and use of its facilities.

2. Free monthly magazine *Camping and Outdoor Life* and the bi-monthly magazine *Caravanning*, the Club's own publication.

3. Free insurance of contents of caravans (subject to certain limits and dates). Special rates are quoted for additional insurances.

4. The opportunity to join the R.A.C. as an associate member at a reduced price.

5. Technical advice on all aspects of caravanning, equipment and sanitation (this advice is also available to members who feel they would like to join the Club, but have not yet decided what sort of outfit to purchase).

6. A sites list revised annually for the British Isles, containing thousands of selected sites and listing the facilities available at each.

7. Guidance and advice for beginners.

8. Special discounts on camping equipment at certain stores.

9. The privilege to use the Camping Club "Members Only" sites throughout the country, and also special holiday and touring sites in selected areas during the summer months.

The Club arranges a nation-wide "Meets" programme containing hundreds of weekend meets, all or any of which members can attend. Major National Club meets are held at the Easter, Whitsun and Autumn Bank Holidays. The Club also organizes winter social activities.

A Club Council and a Club Committee run the Club on behalf of members, and every member of this Council and this Committee is an active mobile caravanner.

MOTOR CARAVANNERS CLUB
5 Dunsfold Rise, Coulsdon, Surrey

The Club was founded in 1960 by a group of enthusiasts who found that their motor caravans were not welcome at either camping (tent) or caravan sites, and not wanted by the established caravan and camping clubs. It caters solely for motor caravanners and claims to be the only club in the world to do so. Its main object is to safeguard the interests of those who camp in motor caravans. Membership is open only to those whose 'vans comply with the standards laid down by the Club. In addition, the Club offers:

1. A list of sites which accept motor caravans.
2. A monthly magazine for members – *The Motor Caravanner.*
3. A special insurance policy available to members at special rates.
4. A home and overseas touring service.
5. Advice on "private conversions".

THE MOTOR CARAVAN SECTION (OF THE CAMPING CLUB OF GREAT BRITAIN AND IRELAND)
11 Lower Grosvenor Place, London S.W.1.

Members receive all the normal advantages of the Camping Club of Great Britain membership, ranging from exclusive sites to technical service. Each spring the Club issues free to its members a 340-page yearbook which, in addition to all other features, lists many hundreds of camp sites with details of the facilities they provide. Members also receive a lively, illustrated monthly magazine *Camping and Outdoor Life*, and that too is free.

There are rallies, national ones, including the Section "Feast of Lanterns" which takes place at the end of each season, and a large number of local meets held in many parts of the country.

National and local rallies provide a splendid opportunity for getting together with like-minded people to examine their various outfits, and discuss gadgets, gimmicks and the ways other 'van enthusiasts solve their problems.

Perhaps you are thinking of touring abroad? The Section organises parties of motor caravanners which tour many countries, including France, Italy, Switzerland and Germany.

For the lone wolves, the Section can provide help and advice on planning their trips overseas. And there are naturally many other services which the Section is rapidly developing. They have, for instance, negotiated an excellent motor caravan insurance policy; they have set up a technical sub-committee, and are collating information on 'vans and conversions and preparing technical notes.

Even if you are not normally an enthusiastic joiner of clubs and societies, it will be well worth your while to join this one! The motor caravanner – legally a caravanner – badly needs a powerful organisation to guard his interests. The Caravan Sites Act has meant that some sites have already been closed to him, whilst suitable tented sites may refuse to accept him because they are not licensed for caravans.

The more you are together the stronger you will be!

Membership is open to all who own a motor caravan. You have to join the Camping Club first, but the additional subscription to the Motor Caravan Section is only a nominal amount.

THE CARAVAN CLUB
46 Brook Street, London W.1

The Caravan Club, which was founded in 1907 in the horse-drawn caravan days, is the oldest club of its kind in the world. It is also the largest, with a membership of over 100 000. From the very beginning it has aimed to enrol only genuine mobile caravanners, and its representation of them and services for them have met with no small measure of success. This is due very largely to the high standards that the Club expects of its members. These are based on the Caravan Code (which appears later in this book), to which all members agree to conform when they apply and are equally required to follow under the terms of the constitution once they are admitted to membership.

Club Sites
In 1967 members had at their disposal over 60 sites managed by the Club and some 700 "certified locations". Many of these are in the national parks and other areas of outstanding beauty, and always suit the person who tours to get away from it all.

Sites Directory and Handbook
The *Sites Directory and Handbook* is issued annually to members free of charge. In addition to the Club sites mentioned, it also lists some 2200 others that are thought to be useful to members, and contains details of the national parks and national forest parks, lists of ferries, notes on the law, and hints and advice on caravanning generally.

Sites Map

Also issued free annually is a road map of Great Britain, folded to fit into the *Sites Directory* and showing all the Club sites and "certified locations", as well as a large number of useful night halts.

Club Life and Centres

For social purposes the Club is divided into fifty local units, known as divisions or centres, each of which arranges a full fixture list of rallies and social events throughout the year.

Protection and Public Relations

The Club has for many years kept a careful watch on any new legislation affecting caravanners, retaining the services of parliamentary agents for this purpose. It has a number of successes to its credit, not the least being its exemption from the Caravanning Sites and Control of Development Act, 1960.

The Club also maintains close relations with such organisations as the National Trust, the Forestry Commission, the Council for the Preservation of Rural England (with its affiliated bodies in Scotland and Wales) and the National Farmers' Union, and co-operates with the Department of the Environment and the planning committees of various national parks and local authorities generally.

The protection of public relations aspect of the Club's work has proved of incalculable value and in itself can be said to justify the mobile caravanner taking out membership of the Club in order to support its efforts.

En Route

As one of its services, the Club supplies to every member a monthly magazine *En Route* which deals with matters of general interest, such as caravan tests, technical and news items, travel reports and Club events.

Foreign Touring Service

The "Red Pennant" Foreign Touring Service of the Club is designed to provide a comprehensive travel, breakdown and accident/sickness insurance service, routes, Customs documents and ferry bookings.

Foreign Touring Handbook

The *Foreign Touring Handbook*, which gives general caravanning information as well as information specific to twenty-six countries, is issued free to members on request besides being automatically included in the Foreign Touring Service.

International Camping Carnet

For a small fee (free if travelling under the Red Pennant Service) the Club will issue members with an International Camping Carnet, which includes Third Party insurance as well as giving access to a large number of sites on the Continent at reduced charges. The Club is a member of the Alliance Internationale de Tourisme and the Federation Internationale de Camping et Caravanning, and is playing an increasingly important part in international caravanning.

Rescue Service

The Club will pay the cost (within the limits set out in the *Sites Directory and Handbook*) of recovering a member's caravan which has become immobile whilst on tour in the United Kingdom.

Free Legal Defence and Assistance

The Club will provide the payment of solicitor's frees within the limits set out in the *Sites Directory and Handbook.*

Technical and Legal Advice

The Club offers free advice on matters to do with mobile caravanning, consulting the Club's solicitors or other experts when necessary.

Insurance

The Club works closely with the Sun Alliance and London Insurance Group, whose caravan policy (the first in the field) was drawn up in consultation with the Club. Expert and impartial advice on all matters connected with insurance is offered to members.

R.A.C. Associate Membership

Caravan Club members can become associate members of the R.A.C. for a reduced annual subscription. The Club has not the facilities to furnish members with detailed routes in the British Isles, a service already amply given by this motoring organisation.

THE TRAILER CARAVAN CLUB
38 Court Parade, East Lane, Wembley, Middlesex

Membership of the Caravan Tourist Association is automatic to those joining the Trailer Caravan Club, which also offers:

1. Free accident insurance.
2. Free legal advice.
3. Regular Club rallies.
4. Special reduced prices for accessories (saving you pounds).
5. Free sites directory, listing more than 2000 night halts.

Appendix B

The Code for Campers

(Reprinted from the Handbook of the Camping Club of Great Britain and Ireland with their kind permission.)

1. *Camp Sites.* Camp on private land in preference to wasteland and do not forget to ask permission. Be careful to conform to any regulations of the site owner and local authority.

2. *Fires.* Do not light any wood fires without permission, or break down hedges or trees for firewood. Avoid lighting fires and throwing down lighted matches or cigarette ends near dry grass or bushes, taking special care in the neighbourhood of forests and plantations. Be very careful in the use of stoves.

3. *Refuse.* Do not leave litter anywhere. If no receptacle is provided, take your rubbish home.

4. *Sanitation.* The utmost care should be taken in matters of sanitation, and campers must conform to the practice laid down in the Camping Club Year-book. The Club's position as the national organisation for camping and caravanning renders correct sanitary methods a duty as well as a necessity. It is essential that the individual member should carry out this duty in such a way as to set a high standard for all campers. The camper who commits a sanitary nuisance not only fails in his duty but also risks

punishment for the site owner and even prohibition from letting the land for further camping.

5. *Country courtesy.* Use courtesy in all your dealings with local people. Their livelihood may be prejudiced by misuse of your privileges. When walking through pasture lands or cultivated fields leave gates, etc., as you find them and take care not to damage crops, wild flowers or woodlands. When camping, seek privacy yourself and respect the privacy of others. Do not sing or play instruments to the nuisance of residents. Study the reasons why country ways are often different from those of the town and always remember your conduct may affect the reception of those campers who follow you.

6. *Regular camp sites.* The individual camper should politely urge that site owners who provide sanitary arrangements should keep these clean, healthy and tidy, and should report to the Camping Club any accommodation which is unsatisfactory or insufficient for the number of persons using the site. Camping Club headquarters will then take the necessary steps.

7. *Occasional camp sites.* When the ground is used only occasionally for camping and the site is not developed commercially, the individual camper is responsible for cleanly conditions. Either the owner's latrine must be used or the camper must provide a latrine in a suitable position.

8. The shelter of a hedge or wall which may offer a safe pitch for some lightweight camper is not a suitable position for a latrine.

Private latrines are generally best placed on the

northern or eastern side of a camping field and well
away from the wall or hedge. Many sites have been
fouled by thoughtlessness or selfish indifference to
the comfort of those who might follow. The site
owner's advice and permission about position should
be obtained.

Minimum precautions. The camper should borrow a
spade or a trowel and dig a shallow hole – where
possible about 8 ins deep – where no inconvenience
can be caused to a subsequent camper. There should
be a screen of trees, bushes or suitable material.
There must be enough loose earth to cover completely the excreta and protect it from flies. Before the
site is left the hole must be filled in and the turf carefully replaced. A covering of stones is insufficient and
insanitary.

Fixed camp. Any camper using a fixed centre for a
week or more must provide a latrine properly
screened. If a camper is to remain several days on a
site the hole should be about 12 ins deep. A suitable
width is 6–8 ins, with a length of 12–18 ins. Loose
earth and a trowel or stick should be kept inside the
erected screen. Proper toilet paper, flat if carried,
rolled if covered and kept in position, should be
used. Other paper is untidy and unhygienic.

Liquid waste. It is considered as important to dispose
of liquid waste as to burn or bury solid rubbish. A
grease pit should have a cover of grass, bracken or the
like which will catch the solid matter and which can
be burnt, and a chemical should be sprinkled in the
pit to discourage insects.

Appendix C

The Caravan Code

(Reprinted from a leaflet published by the Caravan Club with their kind permission.)

1. The Caravan:

   (a) The caravan is a vehicle specifically designed for caravanning and of good appearance. Its colouring and decoration are appropriate and do not antagonise public opinion.
   (b) It is always maintained in sound condition.

2. On the Road:

   (a) The caravan complies with the Road Traffic Acts and Regulations. Its weight distribution and undergear are not such as to cause undesirable swaying.
   (b) The owner ensures that it is insured against Third Party risks and that the car policy is not invalidated by towing.
   (c) The caravanner causes as little inconvenience as possible by looking out for and giving way to faster traffic.
   (d) He allows himself an ample safety margin for stopping or changing direction.
   (e) He keeps close to the left and is careful not to

return too quickly to the left after passing cyclists or other slower traffic.

(f) He does not tow a caravan so large and heavy that the towing car cannot hold it steady under all normal conditions without snaking, or cannot climb ordinary main road hills without failing and obstructing other traffic, or cannot pull up in an adequate distance under braking.

3. On the Site:

(a) The caravanner does not stop on private land without obtaining the permission of the owner.

(b) He places his caravan where it will not interfere with the convenience or enjoyment of others.

(c) He keeps his pitch neat and tidy with no loose equipment outside the caravan beyond what is necessary or appropriate. He leaves his pitch as clean or cleaner than when he found it.

(d) On organised sites he disposes of all rubbish by the means provided, and on casual sites he buries it or takes it away for disposal elsewhere in a proper manner.

(e) He collects waste water from the caravan waste outlet in a receptacle which he does not allow to overflow and foul the ground. On organised sites he disposes of waste water in the manner provided for, and on casual sites he minimises fouling of the ground, e.g. by distributing water along a hedge.

(f) He does not damage the turf by digging unnecessary holes or by the improper use of his car.

(g) For touring he carries his own sanitary equipment, comprising a chemical closet and a suitable fluid. He does not rely on the earth method except for casual sites in very remote country. When the contents of the chemical closet are disposed of by burial, he avoids the vicinity of any watercourse.

(h) At organised sites he keeps his dog under proper control. He drives very slowly through the caravan lines and avoids singing, loud radio and electric generator or other noises at an hour when it would reasonably annoy others.

(i) He makes sure that any laundry necessarily hung outside the 'van is displayed discreetly.

(j) He observes the Country Code relating to fire dangers, litter, gates, damage to crops, hedges, trees or livestock.

4. General:

The caravanner shows courtesy and consideration to all with whom he comes in contact so that the good-will of caravanners is enhanced, and he pays his proper dues.

Appendix D

Useful Addresses

The Camping Club of Great Britain and Ireland, 11 Lower Grosvenor Place, London S.W.1.

The Motor Caravan Section (of the Camping Club of Great Britain and Ireland), 11 Lower Grosvenor Place, London S.W.1.

The Canoe Club, 11 Lower Grosvenor Place, London S.W.1.

The British Caravanners Club, 11 Lower Grosvenor Place, London S.W.1.

All the above are sections of or are associated with the Camping Club of Great Britain and Ireland.

The Auto Camping Club, 51a Chipstead Valley Road, Coulsdon, Surrey.

The Motor Caravanners Club, 5 Dunsfold Rise, Coulsdon, Surrey.

The Caravan Club, 46 Brook Street, London W.1.

Central Council of Physical Recreation, 26/29 Park Crescent, London W.1.

Black & Edgington, 53 Rathbone Place, Oxford Street, London W.1.

The National Parks Commission, 1 Cambridge Gate, London N.W.1.

The Ramblers Association, 124 Finchley Road, London N.W.3.

You've taken the 'quick way' cross-Channel. You've driven hundreds of kilometres.

Now–set up camp.

There's an easier way to the Continent's camp-sites. **Bigger ships. Better route. Time for a real, relaxing, breather on the way. Normandy Car Ferries, Southampton-Le Havre.** The roads are clearer to Southampton. You drive on board your Normandy ferry for the day or night crossing – and relax. Big bar-lounges. Room to stretch and sleep in reclining seats, cabins or couchettes. Cafeteria and restaurant. Sun-deck. Shopping arcade.

It's a real break – and a comfortable one.
And when you drive off at Le Havre, rested and refreshed, you're in camping country already. Or you can carry on down good clear roads to the rest of France, to Spain or Italy.
Camp Equipment Hire—at special low rates. Travel out and return on Normandy Car Ferries, and you can pre-book everything you'll need for your camping holiday *and* save 25% on normal hire charges!

For free brochure, see your Travel Agent or Motoring Organisation, or write to: Normandy Ferries, (TYC), Arundel Towers, Southampton SO9 4AE. Telephone: 0703-32131.

NORMANDY CAR FERRIES
Southampton-Le Havre
The civilised way south to the sun

Normandy Ferries is a service operated by the General Steam Navigation Company Limited, a member of the P&O Group, in association with SAGA, Paris.

The Royal Automobile Club, Touring Service and Caravanning and Camping Service, P.O. Box 92, Cross Road, Croydon, Surrey.

The Irish Tourist Office, 150 New Bond Street, London W.1.

The Bergen Line, 21–24 Cockspur Street, London S.W.1.

The Trailer Caravan Club, 38 Court Parade, East Lane, Wembley, Middlesex.

Big Fleet Car Ferries, 53 Rathbone Place, Oxford Street, London W.1. (An association of British and French Rail and Black & Edgington to provide a first-class ferry and camp hire service.)

Players Sports Ltd. (Camping Suppliers and Hire), 53 Rathbone Place, Oxford Street, London W.1. (Part of the Black & Edgington organisation.)

Townsend Car Ferries (including a camp hire service) – Camp Hire Dept.: P.O. Box No. 12, Dover, Kent; Travel Service: 41 Piccadilly, London W.1.

British United Air Ferries, Portland House, Stag Place, London S.W.1.

Thorenson Car and Passenger Ferries, 127 Regent Street, London W.1.

British Rail Car Carrying Services – apply at the station from which you propose to start. These are as shown in the brochure issued by the British Rail Car Carrying Services, which is available from travel agents and from the Divisional Manager, British Railways, Western Region, Paddington Station, London W.2.

P.T.C. Ltd. (agents in Great Britain for Camping Gaz and tent manufacturers), South Street, Dorking, Surrey.

John Hawley (Walsall) Ltd. (manufacturers of Goodall Tents) Bloxwich Road, Walsall, Staffs.

Appendix E

Useful Tables and Figures

Some Speed Limits Abroad

Austria: 50 km/h in built-up areas.

Belgium: 60 km/h in built-up areas, but watch for local limits.

France: 60 km/h in towns, but local authorities can vary this.

Italy: 50 km/h in built-up areas with local variations.

Luxembourg: 60 km/h in built-up areas.

Holland: 50 km/h in built-up areas. There is a limit on cars towing trailers of over 7 cwts.

Spain: Local limits which vary from town to town.

Switzerland: 60 km/h in built-up areas. 80 km/h elsewhere if you are towing.

West Germany: 50 km/h in built-up areas. Elsewhere 80 km/h if towing.

Yugoslavia: 60 km/h in built-up areas. Elsewhere 120 km/h.

Although these limits are correct at the time of writing, they are subject to change and should be checked with the appropriate National Tourist Office.

Metric Conversions

Kilometres to Miles

1 kilometre	=	·6 miles
2	=	1·2
3	=	1·9
4	=	2·5
5	=	3·1
10	=	6·2
25	=	15·5
50	=	31·1
75	=	46·6
100	=	62·1

Kilogrammes to Pounds

1 kilogramme	=	2·2 lbs
2	=	4·4
3	=	6·6
4	=	8·8
5	=	11·0
6	=	13·2
7	=	15·4
8	=	17·6
9	=	19·8
10	=	22·0

Litres to Gallons

5 litres	=	1·1 gallons
6	=	1·3
7	=	1·5
8	=	1·8
9	=	2·0
10	=	2·2
20	=	4·4
30	=	6·6
40	=	8·8
50	=	11·0

Tyre Pressures

Pounds per square inch to kilogrammes per square centimetre:

20 lbs/in^2	=	1·41 kg/cm^2
22	=	1·55
24	=	1·69
26	=	1·83
28	=	1·97
30	=	2·11
32	=	2·25

Index